RESTORING
THE GREAT BRITAIN

Joe Blake

AVON COUNTY LIBRARY

Class No. L38.31

8/94

Alloc. B1   Suppl. RP

REDCLIFFE
Bristol

D0574085

First published in 1989
by Redcliffe Press Ltd., 49 Park Street., Bristol

© Joe Blake

All rights reserved. No part of this publication
may be reproduced, stored in a retrieval system,
or transmitted, in any form or by any means,
electronic, mechanical, photocopying, recording
or otherwise, without the prior permission
of the publishers.

ISBN 0 948265 83 3

Typeset by The Picador Group
and printed by WBC, Bristol.

Contents

Except where indicated in brackets, the source of the illustration is the S.S. Great Britain Project. All photographs from the S.S. Great Britain Project collection are reproduced by the South West Picture Agency.

Introduction

One morning in 1970 an unusual news item caught my eye; apparently a group of enthusiasts hoped to salvage the hull of an historic ship called the s.s. *Great Britain* from a beach in the Falkland Islands. My study of naval history had taught me something about those far-off islands which would be on everyone's lips again in the early 1980s, but the vessel's name awakened only a dim recollection of an early steamship with a large number of masts.

At the time, my prime preoccupation was my imminent retirement from the Royal Navy after some 32 years, and the unwelcome prospect of unemployment for the first time in my life.

For most of my career I had been concerned with underwater weapons, so my best prospects of a job appeared to be in the armaments industry; but somehow I did not fancy the role of an international salesman of sonar sets and torpedoes.

As the weeks passed and the fateful date drew near, I had no lack of advice as I drafted the story of my life to impress potential employers. It was a story that failed singularly to impress an official in the employment exchange, who thought I might be lucky to land a clerk's job on a minuscule salary!

My daily paper kept me in touch with the progress of the salvage job in the Falklands, so I knew she was homeward bound when a naval friend phoned me with the news that the s.s. *Great Britain* Project Committee was about to seek a suitable person to take charge of the vessel on her arrival in the United Kingdom. Lord Strathcona, recently returned from the Falklands, had suggested employing an ex-Royal Naval officer and my friend wondered if I might be interested.

The possibility of becoming a museum curator – even of a ship – had never occurred to me, but the challenge presented by such a unique undertaking excited my interest. I at once asked for an introduction to the Project. Within days I was interviewed by Lord Strathcona, and shortly after by the Chairman of the Project, Richard Goold-Adams, who offered me the post of Project Officer for a period of six months or longer at a salary slightly higher than the one quoted by the employment exchange.

My last day in the Royal Navy was to be Friday, July 10th, and I had promised my wife a special holiday before I began serious job hunting. I now had to break the news that once again I was to take what the navy calls a 'Pierhead Jump', and start not a new appointment but a fresh career.

1—The Birth of the Great Britain

When the tide surged up the river Avon in the old days, the boatmen of Pill strained on their oars to pull laden sailing ships up to Bristol City Docks. They did it for hundreds of years, until the invention of steam-driven machinery for ships led to the development of paddle tugs. It was a harsh life for those brawny tugmen, especially in winter, but there was still opposition to this change which affected the livelihood of so many.

On a wider front, commercial pressures and the genius of a new breed of engineer combined to introduce steam packets for cross-Channel and coastal services. They were a great boom for the travelling public, accustomed to accepting a timetable dominated by the vagaries of the weather; for the first time passengers could enjoy the convenience of the sort of scheduled service we all take for granted today.

By 1830 steam-powered vessels with paddle wheels had been adopted widely for local and port services, and even the traditionalists of the Royal Navy had bowed to the inevitable and supported the building of an experimental steam-powered warship.

On land, the impact of steam machinery was seen in the rapid proliferation of railways throughout Britain, including a London-to-Bristol line which became known as the Great Western. This introduced the engineer Isambard Kingdom Brunel to the techniques of railroad construction, but his skills far transcended the discipline of civil engineering. This became clear in 1835, when he set the railway directors back on their heels by asking: 'Why not make the line longer, and have a steamboat to go from Bristol to New York, and call it the *Great Western*?' At first the suggestion was treated as a joke, but soon it was discussed more seriously, and a committee was formed to sponsor the project.

This was the somewhat light-hearted manner in which the concept of using steam power for a transatlantic liner service was born, but there was much opposition to be overcome, quite apart from that of the mostly American companies then operating sailing packet services. In particular a Dr Lardner, an acknowledged authority on the economics of steam propulsion, discouraged potential supporters when he 'proved' in a lecture to the British Association that a steam vessel of 1,600 tons could not carry coal enough for more than 2,080 miles. Brunel was at the lecture and tried to expose the errors in the distinguished speaker's calculations. In particular, his own studies, possibly with William Froude, who joined him as an assistant in 1837 and later became a world leader in the science of hydro-dynamics, had taught him that: 'the resistance of vessels in the water does not increase in direct proportion to their tonnage. Tonnage increases as the cubes of their dimensions, while the resistance increases about as their squares; so that a vessel of double the tonnage of another, capable of

5

containing an engine of twice the power, does not really meet with double the resistance, Speed, therefore, will be greater with the large vessel, or the proportionate power of the engine and consumption of fuel may be reduce.' Unfortunately, the truth of his claim was not accepted, or perhaps comprehended, by many of those present; but it is interesting to reflect that, more than 150 years later, today's mammoth tankers amply demonstrate the ultimate economic benefit of heeding Brunel's fundamental observations.

In spite of all such difficulties, the Great Western Steam Ship Company was formed, and it raised sufficient capital for their first keel to be laid down in William Patterson's yard in Bristol in 1836. This large paddle steamer, built of wood but with a number of special iron strengthening features designed by Brunel, was launched in 1838. The *Great Western* provided the first liner service under steam between Bristol and New York, and it was an immediate success. Unhappily, with only one ship, the company could not guarantee a sufficiently frequent or reliable service to win the mail contract, but investors were soon queuing to subscribe for more shares in the company to fund a second vessel.

At first the construction of a sister ship to the *Great Western* was considered, but Brunel pressed the need for a larger vessel. A major problem was the fact that wood was unsuitable for a ship of much more then 2,000 tons displacement, but the master engineer swept this aside with the momentous suggestion that the new vessel should be built wholly of iron. At that time a few small ships and barges had been made in this way and were

operating successfully, but the material had yet to be accepted for hulls for open ocean services, where far greater strains would be imposed on them by heavy seas. As momentous as Brunel's idea was the Great Western Steam Ship Company board's decision to back it, and the lines of a hull displacing some 3,000 tons were drawn by William Patterson.

Brunel applied his engineering skills to prepare a specification that took account of the endless stresses imposed on a vessel in heavy weather, and the success of his design is demonstrated not only by the survival of the ship to the present day, but by the incorporation of many of his design features in every iron and steel ship from then until today. This lead to that pioneering vessel, which was of course named the *Great Britain*, being described as the grandmother of modern shipping.

So the company faced the task of building what was then to be the largest ship in the world by using materials never previously used in regular shipbuilding yards. Moreover, the size of the hull was far too great for any existing building slips, so it was decided to construct the ship in a building dock. The company had established a repair yard, to include a dock then in the process of excavation, on the southern side of Bristol harbour about a quarter of a mile to the west of William Patterson's yard at Prince's Wharf. It was decided to adapt this repair yard to build the new iron ship, facing up bravely to the considerable extra costs. In particular, the dry dock had to be enlarged and realigned, so that the new ship could be floated out without hitting the wall on the other side of the harbour.

At last the preparations were complete, and construction began with the laying of the keel plates in July 1839. At the time, this was probably the largest single object in the world to be built wholly of wrought iron, and the preparation and transport of materials must have posed many problems. It seems that the total of some 1,200 tons of iron plate and sections was bought from the Coalbrookdale Iron Company in Staffordshire and shipped in by barge using the rivers Severn and Avon.

The ship was ready for launching, or floating out, in 1843, and it has been suggested that four years was an inordinately long building time. But it must be remembered that not only was the vessel being made of a relatively new shipbuilding material, with an inevitable shortage of necessary skills and frequent delays in solving novel technical problems, but a fundamental change in the hull resulted from a decision, during building, to introduce screw propulsion. As laid down the ship was to have paddle wheels, but in early 1840 the merits of screw propulsion were demonstrated by a vessel called *Archimedes*, fitted with a screw propeller designed by Francis Pettitt Smith. Brunel was sufficiently impressed to recommend that the building of the *Great Britain* should be stopped until he had carried out trials on the *Archimedes*, and the results of these convinced him of the overwhelming superiority of the screw. To their credit, the company and its money men readily agreed to this fundamental change in design.

Apart from obvious alterations to the hull, the propulsion machinery had to be turned through 90 degrees to transmit power via a shaft running the length of the after hold. The engineer Humphreys had been engaged to develop a scaled-up version of his patent trunk engine to drive the ship, but this was now too large to fit in the changed position. Possibly as a result of the stresses involved, he suffered 'brain fever' and died, leaving Brunel with neither engine nor designer. At this time very low steam pressures had to be used at sea as only salt water was available for the boilers, so engines were only a step removed from the atmospheric design, and very slow-moving. This was ideal for paddle wheels, but it meant that gearing was essential to increase the speed of propeller shaft revolutions.

Never at a loss, Brunel developed his own engine based on an earlier design by his father, a 'triangle engine' for paddle propulsion. In this, a pair of cylinders mounted at the bottom of the vessel formed an inverted V, with the crankshaft above. To produce the necessary power two pairs of cylinders were introduced, mounted in the turn of the bilge to port and starboard. They drove a crankshaft running fore and aft at the upper 'tween deck level, and to transmit movement to the propeller shaft and give it a higher speed of rotation, Brunel first experimented with straps or belts. Finally he adopted a system similar to that used in bicycles today—a novel design of toed chain, meshing with hardwood slats around the large upper and small lower chain wheels.

At length all was completed, and in successful trials in the Bristol Channel in January 1845, a speed of more than 12 knots was achieved using the engine alone.

A few days later the ship sailed

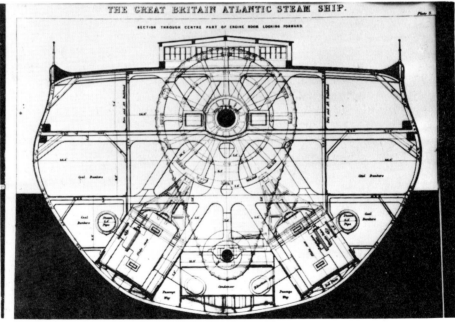

Top: The Great Britain fitting out in Bristol—1844. (An original photograph by Fox Talbot held by National Maritime Museum)

Bottom: A contemporary engraving of a cross section through the engine room.

on her maiden voyage to London, straight in to the teeth of a gale. The famous marine artist Joseph Walter was a passenger, and one of his best-known paintings is of a large wave breaking over her bows. The hull suffered some trivial damage, but the engine worked steadily and the voyage was completed without further incident.

The ship stayed in the port of London until June 12, and among an endless stream of visitors was the Queen herself. This was an extraordinarily long stay for a purely public relations exercise, and it seems likely that the interior decorations and furnishings had to be finished, using the London firms that had worked so successfully on the *Great Western*.

While the *Great Western* was being built, the port of Liverpool was growing to meet the needs of the new transatlantic steamers so much so that by 1845 the Great Western Steam Ship Company had decided to turn away from Bristol, where many disadvantages included heavy port dues, and make Merseyside its United Kingdom terminal. So it was to Liverpool that the *Great Britain* headed from London, and from there she made her first voyage to New York on July 26, 1845.

By August 1846 four successful round trips had been completed, and in spite of the lack of a mail contract there was every prospect of a profit for the company. Like the *Great Western*, this revolutionary new vessel suffered very few technical defects, and the reliability of the line's service and its high standards of comfort and catering were beginning to establish the sort of reputation that attracts customers.

Then disaster struck! On the night of September 22, 1846, outward bound to New York, the *Great Britain* grounded on a shingle beach at Dundrum Bay on the North-east coast of Ireland.

Much has already been written about this tragic event, but suffice it to say that it resulted from a series of navigational blunders which reflected no credit on her captain and officers. On the other hand, the survival of her hull, relatively undamaged, spoke eloquently of the skill of her designers and builders, and helped establish the superiority of iron as a material for building ships.

After nearly a year stranded on the shore the ship was refloated and towed back to Merseyside, but there was no happy ending for her owners. Under-insured and already carrying substantial debts, they were forced into liquidation and had to offer both vessels for sale. Not surprisingly, there was not a rush of bidders for the *Great Britain*. She was a sorry sight, lying in port bearing all the evidence of a year's neglect on an exposed shore, and in the background there were the unknown problems of maintaining an iron hull with screw propulsion.

It was not until December 1850, after languishing in Birkenhead for more than three years, that she was bought by Gibbs, Bright and Co. for £18,000. This was about a sixth of her original cost five years previously.

What clinched the sale was the discovery of gold in Australia, leading to a clamour for passages to that continent, but the *Great Britain* had one major snag. She had been designed for the Atlantic, and carried coal for only about 3,000 miles' continuous steaming. There was a lack of coaling stations between England

and Australia, so the new owners were faced with the task of converting her from a steamship with auxiliary sails into a sailing ship with auxiliary steam. Brunel's engine and boilers, which had suffered corrosion damage and more in the Dundrum Bay grounding, were replaced, the new engine being a two-cylinder model by Penn. To reduce the drag of the propeller when the engine was idle, a clutch was fitted so that the screw could revolve freely, and above decks two telescopic funnels could be lowered while sailing to reduce wind resistance. The sailing rig was altered with four masts, two of them square-rigged, but in service the sail area soon proved to be barely adequate.

With voyages of about 60 days and a demand for cheap accommodation, passenger arrangements also had to be revised. A long deckhouse above the weather deck provided a first class saloon, and the original dining saloons were given over to cargo and steerage passengers.

After a single voyage to the United States, the ship began her long series of passages to Australia in 1852. The new engine performed well, but there was some doubt about the value of the telescopic funnels and the sailing clutch proved hazardous. Then came the Crimean War, and a period of government charter which at least kept the money men happy. At the end of it, in 1857, there was an extensive refit in which she became a full-rigged ship with square sails on three large masts. Other major changes included the removal of the sailing clutch and the installation of a lifting propeller trunk complete with a two-bladed Griffiths screw and clutch mechanism.

By 1876 many new vessels were appearing on the liner routes, and the *Great Britain* was becoming uneconomic. She was laid up at Birkenhead and seemed destined for the scrapyard, but world trade began to boom again, and everything that floated was pressed into service. Now it made sense to convert this aged passenger liner into a cargo vessel to transport bulk materials under sail alone, and it was a *Great Britain* stripped of all her passenger cabins and steam machinery that sailed under new ownership with a cargo of Welsh coal for the Western United States in 1882. Deep laden well below her original water line, she sailed badly and was ill suited to tackle the severe weather of the South Atlantic, especially around the Horn. She completed two round trips with cargo, but on her third outward voyage with coal she hit exceptionally fierce weather and spent some six weeks struggling to round the Horn. There was some rigging damage and a minor fire in the cargo, and with the crew exhausted almost to the point of mutiny, Captain Stap made a wise decision when he put back to the Falkland Islands for repairs.

At Port Stanley a survey revealed substantial storm damage, most of it beyond the scope of local repair facilities. The owners' decision was to cut their losses, write the ship off as a constructional loss 'beyond economical repair' and negotiate the sale of her hull and cargo to the Falkland Islands Company. So, in 1886, began the final phase of the working life of the *Great Britain*, as a floating store house for coal and wool in Port Stanley harbour.

She played the part well for 50 years, but at last the company

Top: Crossing the Atlantic under steam and sail. (A modern painting by K.A. Griffin)

Bottom: After the 1857 refit with three masts for the continuing service to Australia.

decided that her working days must end. The question of what happened next led to the formation of a group determined to save her because of her historical importance, but Europe was only slowly recovering from recession, and gathering war clouds meant that not too many people's thoughts were on decaying hulks on the other side of the world. Had there been a scrapyard in Stanley, that would undoubtedly have been the end of the story, but the nearest one was so far away that the cost of towing, with its attendant risks, could not be justified. The possibility of using the hull as a target for naval gunfire until it sank in deep water was also considered, but not followed up by the Admiralty. Finally, in 1937, it was decided to tow the ship from Port Stanley harbour to Sparrow Cove, where she was beached, holed to flood the interior, and left to rot, a rough-and-ready compromise that offered little hope for the future. Indeed, it was 30 years before fate again intervened, in the form of a letter to *The Times* in November 1967. Dr Ewan Corlett, an eminent naval architect, called attention to the survival of the hull and concluded with these words: 'May I make a plea that the authorities should at least document, photograph, and fully record this wreck and at best do something to recover the ship and place her on display as one of the very few really historic ships still in existence.'

This letter galvanised a group of enthusiasts determined to support Dr Corlett in his aims, and so began a campaign which defied the odds and not only salvaged the ship but brought her home to her very birthplace, the Great Western Dock in Bristol.

2—The Rescue

In the Falkland Islands the stranded hull of the Great Britain was a popular target for boat trips, and there is no lack of photographs of her in Sparrow Cove. Ignoring the hazard of rotting decks, many intrepid visitors boarded to take a last look at the ship that had been a feature of Port Stanley as long as older inhabitants could remember. Although she had not started to break up, there was a major crack in the starboard side below an opening which had been cut to load wool, and local opinion agreed that the ship's bottom had rusted through.

Against this background the Great Britain Project raised funds to finance a professional survey by Dr Corlett, whose visit to the islands fortunately coincided with a call by H.M.S. *Endurance*. The Ministry of Defence allowed her diving team to help with the underwater survey of the hull, and Dr Corlett was happy to disprove local opinion and report that the vessel could be made sufficiently watertight to float again. But to return her to England would involve a voyage to the other side of the world, and few believed that she was equal to the ordeal.

Various salvage companies were consulted, and proposals to sustain buoyancy suggested everything from air bags to ping-pong balls. Few seemed interested in tendering for such an unusual and risky venture, but then it was discovered that Ulrich Harms of Hamburg had developed a new technique for transporting damaged vessels back to a repair yard. In effect, this enabled a casualty to be 'docked' on a floating pontoon which could then be towed anywhere in the world. An investigation proved that the pontoon was just big enough to accommodate the *Great Britain*, at a keel length of 285 feet and an estimated weight of 1,200 tons. The cost of hiring this equipment was then about £800 a day, so a major fund-raising effort would obviously be required. Fortunately the project then received the support of the Bristol-born millionaire Jack Hayward, whose guarantee of £150,000 meant that at last the salvage attempt could begin. The firm of Risdon-Beazley in Southampton was contracted for the salvage, and Ulrich Harms arranged for a pontoon completing work in West Africa to go on to the South Atlantic.

In March 1970 work began in Sparrow Cove to refloat the stranded hull. To reduce weight the salvage team removed the three huge wooden masts installed in 1857, some of the largest ever built, and holes cut in the hull plating near the stern were sealed, along with other obvious leaks.

Then attention was concentrated on the crack in the starboard side. Using divers, the salvage engineer arranged for a number of hair mattresses brought in from Port Stanley to be rammed in the gap; it was expected that when the ship floated, the crack would tend to close and the gap would be sealed by the mattresses, and so it proved. Finally the pumps were started, and on April 7 the *Great Britain* was afloat once more.

Beached at Sparrow Cove in the Falkland Islands. (Photograph: Marion Morrison)

Meanwhile, the pontoon was prepared, with a row of blocks for the wooden keel. A level area of sea bed was selected near by, and the pontoon was sunk carefully so that only the large stanchions along each side protruded from the water. The ship was then manoeuvred gently over the pontoon by tugs, and held precisely above the keel blocks. Then, using air pressure, the tanks forming the hull of the pontoon were progressively emptied of water, until the structure rose from the sea bed with the *Great Britain* safely aboard.

The pontoon and its precious cargo were towed across the bay to Stanley, where many Falkland Islanders gathered to renew acquaintance with their old friend. In a formal ceremony on the quayside the Governor, representing the Crown, conveyed the ownership of the aged hull to the Great Britain Project, and with that the ship was free to leave the waters of the colony.

On April 24, 1970, after the vessel had been thoroughly secured, the strange assemblage was towed from Port Stanley for Montevideo. *En route* a severe gale was weathered safely, but at Montevideo it was thought wise to add some extra securing chains to lock the salvaged hull rigidly to the pontoon for the long voyage across the Atlantic. So the final stage of the rescue began and the media, sensing success, began to take an increasingly close interest in the progress of the little flotilla. As it approached British shores helicopters hovered above, and there was tremendous excitement at sea level when the ocean passage ended in a blaze of publicity in Barry Roads, South Wales. Here the tow was transferred to a local tug, which took on the leg of the journey up the Bristol Channel to Avonmouth Docks.

When it became clear that the salvage was likely to succeed, the project had to complete negotiations for a resting place for the hull. History suggested Bristol and by chance her original building dock, then called Wapping Dock, was a feature of the City Docks waterfront, being operated commercially by Charles Hill and Sons. That company offered to accept the ship free of dock charges, on the understanding that all repair work was placed with it. After this all that was needed was the blessing of the Bristol City Council, who owned and operated the City Docks and were concerned that this rusting monster might sink before reaching the dock or end up as a white elephant, one of a happy band of worthy causes supported by the hard-pressed ratepayers.

By the time the pontoon reached Avonmouth it had been agreed that the ship should return to Wapping Dock, but the city council remained adamant that she could stay for only three years. Now began the final phase of the salvage, in which the ship would re-enter the water to be hauled up the river Avon into the City Docks.

The city council, with responsibilities for both the docks and navigation of the Avon, not surprisingly demanded that the project should arrange adequate insurance to cover this final voyage.

Traditionally, marine insurance is placed with Lloyds, and the underwriters require evidence that the ship is fit to undertake the voyage. So it was that the senior Lloyds surveyor in Bristol was called upon to perform one of the most unusual tasks of his career, and to sign a certificate stating that the ship was seaworthy enough to complete the envisaged movement. Wisely, he ordered some additional stiffening across the crack in the hull, and it was properly sealed; compressed mattresses do not feature in the list of fitments acceptable to Lloyds!

Throughout the maritime history of Britain, the weather frequently takes a hand to foil the best-laid plans. The final voyage was scheduled for Saturday, July 4, 1970 and everything was prepared for the great day. There was a mass of advance publicity, and through the morning the crowds were gathering to watch the historic event. Unhappily, an Atlantic depression had built up, and when by mid-day the wind was gusting to more than 40 knots, the pilot abandoned the venture. That evening various pre-planned celebration parties went ahead in an atmosphere of anti-climax, and the weather prospects showed no sign of improving.

On the following morning a lull in the gale prompted the pilot to seize the opportunity to sail, even though conditions were far from ideal for the tow of a dead ship with neither motive power nor an operable rudder. The *Great Britain's*

Top: The pontoon lifting The Great Britain from the sea. (Photograph: Marion Morrison)

Bottom: First sighting from the air approaching the Bristol Channel. (Photograph: Press Association)

luck prevailed, and the voyage was completed without a hitch. This time there was little advance publicity, but vantage points beside the Avon and the City Docks were packed with dense crowds, and the media were out in force.

In the City Docks the ship was berthed at Canon's Marsh on the north side, to await the completion of preparations to receive her back at her original birthplace.

Visitors were not allowed on board but many thousands, includ-ing myself, went to view the vessel as she floated alongside. At first glance she was simply a rusting, perforated hulk in imminent danger of sinking, but close inspection revealed to the practised eye an incredibly strong interior structure likely to be well able to respond to restoration. The underwater section of the hull was amazingly watertight, and only one salvage pump working intermittently was needed to keep her dry.

Re-entering Bristol City Docks after an absence of 125 years. (Photograph:
The Graham Farr Collection)

3—The Docking

By the time the *Great Britain* had reached Avonmouth I had begun to meet other members of the project team, though my appointment as project officer was not to take effect until July 13, three days after my retirement from the Royal Navy. Lord Strathcona had represented the project during the salvage operation in the Falklands, and in his absence his wife played an active part in supervising the preparation of the dry dock area to receive and control a sudden influx of visitors.

Although the dock had been in service continuously, in latter years it had been used only spasmodically for the routine docking of small craft, and many supporting workshops had fallen into disuse. The stonework of the dock, which dated from the 1830s, was in fair condition, and better still, the floor was still reasonably even and certainly able to support the weight of the original occupant. The dock gate, or caisson, had been replaced in 1928 and provided a fairly watertight seal, while an automatic pump kept the dock dry. In case the entrance had been altered since 1845 a careful check was made to ensure that the ship could still pass through, and then three rows of dock blocks were set in position to support the main keel and the two side or docking keels. By this time the ship had arrived at Avonmouth, so measurements from the original drawings could be checked in case her keels had been altered significantly during service. Research also revealed that the water level of the floating

harbour had had to be raised by about eighteen inches to float the ship out of the dock in 1843, and it was clear that a similar increase in depth would be needed to float her clear above the dock blocks.

The level of Bristol City Docks is maintained by water from the rivers Avon and Frome. During spring tides the level is below sea level, so it could be raised if the port authority allowed the tidal waters to enter the docks via the Cumberland Basin. The earliest date for a spring tide likely to achieve the required level was on the evening of Sunday, July 19—by great good fortune, the anniversary of the ship's launch in 1843.

Plans were laid and Prince Philip, who had encouraged the project throughout the salvage, said he wished to be present for the docking. Again the project found itself with a full-scale media event on its hands, and the tugmen and shipyard workers found themselves carrying out this unique and tricky piece of seamanship in an unaccustomed glare of publicity.

When the ship was built her bows were at the west, or entrance, end of the dock, and it was decided to replace her in the same way, in spite of the fact that ships are normally docked 'bows in'. A hidden benefit was that this presented an increasingly striking view of the ship from across the water, as restoration progressed.

The docking went ahead after some early doubts whether the harbour level would reach the required

The original Great Western Dock prepared to receive its first-born.
(Photograph: Richard Goold-Adams)

height. Tugs manoeuvred the unwieldy hull into position to enter the dock, and lines were then passed to two tractors on each side. As they gently pulled her through the entrance it was clear that the addition of wood cladding to the outside of the hull plating in 1882, had reduced the clearance on each side to inches; the stonework on the south side was scraped, and civic dignitaries and other guests were showered with shellfish and weed as they pushed against the old hull in an effort to ease its passage!

By the time the dock gate had been replaced it was dark. The sluice was opened so that the dock would be drained as the tide fell, and as the *Great Britain* settled slowly on the dock blocks there were sounds of stress in her aged structure.

They culminated when suddenly, from within her hull, came a deep groan followed by complete silence; it was as if the old bones had found perfect comfort and peace at last.

So another piece of British industrial history had been saved for posterity; but it remained to be seen whether there would be the public interest to raise the funds to conserve and restore Brunel's revolutionary vessel.

4—Flooded With Visitors

While the *Great Britain* was *en route* from the Falklands, the important decision was made to allow visitors to view the hull as soon as possible after docking. This raised the problems of access, safety, basic amenities and car parking, and all were tackled energetically by Lady Strathcona.

By 1970 the original offices of the Great Western Steam Ship Company and much of its yard had been taken over by a timber merchant. Access to the dock area for Charles Hill and Sons' workmen was provided by a wicket gate from their yard next door, but the only way in from Gas Ferry Road was via a right of way through the woodyard. Neither route was convenient or acceptable for public use, but happily there was a long-disused access to the old towpath running along the harbour edge to the north of the dock. A new doorway was cut through the corrugated iron wall of a disused workshop, a way was hacked through the brambles and nettles of the towpath, and the result was a footpath from Gas Ferry Road.

Safety provision at that stage was centred on improving the fencing around the dry dock, but in succeeding years the project has kept all aspects of public well-being at the top of the agenda.

As for basic amenities, the inherited toilet facilities at the dock—male only!—were a period piece consisting of an iron-panelled enclosure dating from the last century. This has been widely admired from the outside and is now the subject of a preservation order, but for a number of years it provided a more pressing service for our gentlemen visitors! Provision for ladies had never been envisaged, but we adapted an existing toilet beside a small workshop to offer minimal facilities.

In 1970 Wapping or the Great Western Dock, as it was originally called and was shortly to be renamed, was in a commercial area far removed from Bristol's busy shopping areas. It was not on a regular bus route, and we assumed that most of our visitors would arrive by car or coach. But would they find us? To the rescue came the Automobile Association, who put up temporary signs all over the city, signs which stayed for many years, until they were replaced by standard directions. So complex is the road network of central Bristol, however, that even today some of our visitors get lost. Asking local citizens rarely helps, since even now only a minority have visited the ship, and most tend to associate it with Hotwells, the area from which it can best be viewed across the harbour.

On my first day at the yard, Monday, July 13, 1970, most of the preparations had been completed. As the only permanent member of staff I was introduced to a small suite of offices at the south-west corner of the dockyard, tucked away from the planned public entrance.

Since I found a desk, a chair and an operational G.P.O. telephone, I was up and running! A number of students had been interviewed, and some had been taken on to help with the visitors during their summer vacations, but none was scheduled to report for duty until the following Monday, the day after the anticipated docking.

My only previous experience of welcoming the British public on board ships was during Navy Days, and suddenly I found myself feeling rather like a captain asked to open his ship to visitors the day after he had given his entire ship's company leave! I rushed around opening a bank account, buying account books and a second-hand safe and trying to anticipate all the problems likely to arise from the arrival of numbers of visitors.

Of course, there was a limit to the amount of improvisation I could achieve in such a short time, and when the gate was opened on Tuesday, July 21, just two days after the ship's arrival, hordes of people descended upon us. Our initial attempts at control were overwhelmed, and for a few days we waived the set two shillings for entry, and simply invited visitors to make free will offerings in collecting boxes.

For the voyage up the Avon, walkways made from scaffolding tubes and planks had been laid around the weather deck on top of the rotting woodwork, and we decided to allow visitors to inspect the vessel from these improvised platforms. An inspector from the local authority had less confidence in the strength of the ship's beams than did our naval architect, however, and we had to limit the number of visitors on board to 20. In an effort to control the numbers we charged an extra two shillings, but even so the queues that formed each day along the dockside were lengthy, albeit usually patient and understanding. Eventually the local authority conceded that the ship's structure could withstand greater loads, and the restriction on numbers was lifted.

Many thought that the arrival of the ship would be a nine days' wonder, and that the public would soon lose interest in 'this heap of rusting iron', as she was described by a civic leader. Even some members of our project had envisaged that visitors would not arrive in numbers until the restoration had been largely completed, and with this in mind the early attention of the committee had been focused mainly on restoration plans and funding.

But as the weeks passed and the flood of visitors showed no sign of abating, it became essential to build a small but permanent organisation in Bristol to manage the daily openings. An original plan to close on Mondays and Tuesdays was quickly abandoned, and from those early days visitors have been admitted every day of the year except for Christmas Eve, Christmas Day and the odd day of closure enforced by heavy snow.

After the first few weeks of improvisation we established a small management team consisting of a commercial manager, an office manager and myself as project officer, with one invaluable secretary. By telephoning various large firms in the city we gathered donations of old office furniture sufficient for our needs, and our only purchase was a better second-hand safe. To control the visitors we engaged a small permanent work force who manned a pay kiosk at the entrance, operated a sales point for postcards and souvenirs, carried out safety patrols and provided car park attendants.

At this time the project's head office was in London, where the general secretary was established with the primary aim of raising funds for resto-

Visitors queueing to go aboard. (Photograph: Richard Goold-Adams)

ration. Based on the experience of other charities, the committee then established the project as a company limited by guarantee, to be known as s.s. Great Britain Project Ltd.; a subsidiary commercial company, s.s. Great Britain Trading Ltd., was set up to cover the exhibition activities in Bristol. The commercial manager and I were appointed executive directors of the latter, the activities of which became increasingly independent of the London office. All the profits from the trading company are covenanted annually to the project, and over the years these contributions from visitors have formed a significant part of the restoration budget.

Almost from the opening day we resolved to offer souvenirs to our visitors, and our first sales point was a trestle table with a small selection of postcards and some early publications.

In particular I recall a pamphlet entitled *History and Return Salvage Operations*, published and printed at the expense of the Bristol Junior Chamber of Commerce and Shipping to satisfy the immediate need.

As our first winter approached we began experimental improvements in our operating arrangements, starting with the use of a small hut, previously a timekeeper's office, as a pay box strategically placed at the dock entrance. Next we were fortunate to be given a small sectional hut which was adapted to become a sales kiosk for souvenirs and postcards. Refreshments had been organised from the start by granting a licence to a local trader who for months sold all manner of fare from vans parked in an open-fronted building previously used as a workshop.

The project council that had by now replaced the earlier committee rightly channelled the slender resources available to the preservation of the ship, and this led to an infectious habit of improvisation and self-help among the management and staff of the trading company. By the end of the first six months it was apparent that the ship was becoming a permanent tourist attraction, and that we would have to try to establish more lasting and attractive visitor arrangements in the dockyard.

Using our own labour during the winter, we introduced turnstiles and barriers at the original ticket office and then adapted a small low-ceilinged workshop as the first souvenir shop. Refreshment sales were improved by building a sales kiosk in the large shed and from this, for a period, we provided our own food and drink service. The final stage in setting up our structure came in 1973, when we obtained the lease of the recently closed dock workers' canteen on Wapping Wharf, just outside our entrance; this became the s.s. Great Britain Restaurant, run by a contractor appointed by us.

Of all the facilities demanded by visitors, the provision of a car park caused the most headaches. When the ship arrived, Bristol City Docks were still operating commercially, and the obvious parking area on the adjacent Wapping Wharf could not be used for visitors' cars. Permission was granted

for us to park a few staff cars there, but with this privilege came a hidden hazard. The entrance gates were locked each evening at 5 p.m., before which cars had to be moved into Gas Ferry Road, with its yellow lines effective until 6. Fortunately for us, the traffic wardens had other matters on their minds at that time of day. As for visitors, the city council recognised the demand and offered temporary space in a recently vacated timber yard in Mardyke Ferry Road, about ten minutes' walk from the ship. As we had to provide staff to supervise this site and a small charge was levied, we investigated every piece of open ground in the neighbourhood. It seemed our prayers were answered when we were allowed to use an area of land owned by British Rail beside the Wapping sidings in Gas Ferry Road, but alas, this happy arrangement had to be terminated when a B.R. customer needed a coal pound, and within months we had no car park at all. We approached the port authority in the hope that the now almost disused wharf at Wapping might be allocated, but in vain; for several months the traffic wardens made a killing from our visitors' cars parked illegally in Gas Ferry Road.

In desperation we wrote formally to the city council, who first suggested that visitors should park in Canon's Marsh, some 25 minutes' walk away. Then came a meeting at which the port authority agreed, at last, to the lease of an area of Wapping Wharf, and for the last time we laid out a car park. It seemed sensible to offer free parking, thus saving the cost of attendants, and this was the final stage in the provision of visitor facilities that remained largely unchanged for some ten years.

5—Getting Started

As soon as it was clear that the salvage operation was likely to be successful, the project committee began to make plans for the *Great Britain*'s restoration. These were complicated by several factors, not least the numerous changes that had been made to the ship during her long life, and the almost total neglect of the hull for nearly 80 years.

When the ship became a storage hulk in the Falklands in 1886, both her passenger accommodation and steam machinery had long since been removed. She now lost all but her lower masts and main yard, and suffered some further minor changes to help with the handling of the bales of wool stored on board. After the decision to beach her in Sparrow Cove in 1937 it was only natural that she should first be stripped of everything that could be used elsewhere in the islands. All the original heavy planking of the 'tween decks was removed, and the final traces of cabins and other interior features disappeared into numerous homesteads. The result was the gutted shell rescued from oblivion in 1970.

Naturally, there were protagonists for almost all the restoration options, ranging from a total rebuild of the vessel as launched in 1843 to the simple preservation of the hull more or less as recovered. After careful consideration was given to all the significant events in the ship's life, it was concluded that its most important features were its original concept and technological innovations, which combined to represent such a major leap forward in ship construction and propulsion. As a result, it was decided that the aim of the restoration should be to preserve and restore the external hull as closely as possible to her original maiden voyage condition, and to recreate sufficient of the 1845 interior to show the living conditions for passengers and crew. Later it was decided to build and instal a full-scale replica of the main engine, so that the magnitude of the technological achievement could be appreciated to the full.

Dr Ewan Corlett, who had triggered the whole project by his letter to *The Times* in 1967, had been accumulating copies of every drawing and scrap of information that had survived in libraries, museums, private collections and archives throughout the world, and as a professional naval architect, he was well placed to prepare a set of drawings and a specification for the basic restoration task. By the time the ship reached Bristol most of these were to hand, and provided an invaluable brief for the task that lay ahead.

Soon after the ship had docked a meeting was held between members of the project and the management of Charles Hill and Sons, the repairers, to draw up plans for the preservation and restoration of the hull. At this time Bristol City Council was insisting that the ship must be moved elsewhere in some three years, when a major development of the City Docks area was scheduled to start, so one of our most important requirements was to maintain the hull in a floatable condition.

Because of the many alterations to the ship during its long and varied working life, the restoration of its 1843 arrangement was not a simple matter of repair and replacement. Regular research work had to be carried out on board to relate the evidence remaining in the existing structure to the detail shown in Dr Corlett's drawings, and it quickly became obvious that many structural alterations would be involved throughout the programme. These would require additional drawings for the repairers, and led us to employ a part-time draughtsman at the dock.

But our ambitious plans depended ultimately on the availability of funds. The project had been able to raise the cash for the salvage and voyage home thanks to the generosity of innumerable firms and individuals headed by Sir Jack Hayward, but after the ship had docked in Bristol and all the bills had been paid, less than £20,000 remained in the bank.

Based on our naval architect's specification, an outline of the whole restoration programme prepared in our London office was costed at £650,000, optimistically spread over a period of three years! But down at the coal face in Bristol it quickly became apparent that the speed of advance would be much slower, and our guiding maxim became those well known lines from *Alice in Wonderland*: 'Begin at the beginning, go on till you come to the end; then stop!' In fact it was well that we did not try to rush ahead on borrowed money, because our initial fundraising experience was most disappointing, and we might have found ourselves simply using income to pay loan interest.

Among our hidden benefactors were Charles Hill and Sons, who offered their services on interest-free credit up to £30,000, to be paid off as donations came in. This enabled all the early, unrewarding work of clearing out the bilges and providing safe routes for visitors to go ahead without delay.

Visitors had not at first been seen as a major source of income, although it was hoped that after the ship had been restored their pounds would cover ongoing maintenance. But in the light of our financial position, it became clear to us in Bristol that the income from visitors was crucial, and it was essential for us to keep our overheads, especially labour costs, to an absolute minimum. As a result a net profit was made each year from the very beginning, in spite of the fact that annual visitor numbers declined for the first three years to a low of under 90,000 in 1973.

In those early days the winters were especially depressing, as the rain poured through the rotting weather deck and rust seemed to appear faster than we could remove it to coat the ancient ironwork. Conditions ashore were almost as bad, with improvised facilities in run-down buildings, and looking back I marvel at the loyalty of all our staff, who accepted their lot cheerfully at a very modest rate of pay.

As for me, there were times when I had doubts, but I never despaired. We clearly owned a piece of national treasure, and in the long term we could be assured of public support. Perhaps the turning point for me was a snowy winter's day when nine people paid to view our dripping, rusty monster—and all were

25

thrilled with what they saw.

When the project committee was originally formed and made the momentous decision to attempt the salvage, Richard Goold-Adams had been elected chairman. With the ship's return to Bristol and the establishment of a project council he became its first chairman, and played an active part in laying down the policy for the ongoing management of the project. His wise experience and cautious approach to problems were often called upon, and did much to maintain morale in times of difficulty.

6—Pioneering Days

As work on the hull began in earnest in 1971, the problem of the safety of our visitors had to be kept uppermost in our minds. Charles Hill's workmen were not accustomed to the presence of spectators in the yard, and our staff had to improvise barriers and temporary signs almost daily to ensure that visitors could not stray into danger areas. Inevitably, workmen moved barriers from time to time without replacing them, and this could lead to some heart-stopping situations. I well recall escorting an elderly lady back along a narrow workman's scaffold which she had thought was the way out. But the record shows that apart from the odd bruise or cut through bumping against low beams, our accident book would probably stand comparison with that of any exhibition site in the country.

Of course, there is a price to be paid for combining repair work with visitors, the extra effort that has to be devoted to both planning and scheduling. Each new task called for adjustments to walkways or safety barriers which reached a peak during the re-laying of the weather deck. Perhaps it was lucky that our income did not allow more rapid progress to be made. As a result there was never any pressure to close the ship to visitors, with its inevitable public relations repercussions.

Another factor affecting visitors was the congestion in our cramped yard. Heavy loads enter by the south gate and a large vehicle al-most blocks the road way, and if the crane has to be operated there is the additional hazard of suspended loads and the need for yet more temporary barriers and safety sentries to guide visitors. Restoration work which involves the movement of heavy objects such as masts has always been planned for the winter months, when fewer visitors are around.

Our reward for this extra effort has been a steady flow of enthusiastic callers throughout the year. Many seem as interested in the work in progress as in the ship herself, and we soon realised that all our staff must be trained to answer their questions. Even a purchase in the souvenir shop often leads to a conversation about some feature of the ship or its restoration. Since many people began coming year after year, there were sometimes complaints that 'last year you said that such-and-such would be completed by now!' Partly to offset this, I organised an information board with details of restoration plans, including the programme for the current month.

There were occasional incidents in those early days to lighten the monotony. In particular I recall a security man who was deaf. At the end of the day he was responsible for seeing the last visitors out of the yard, after which he locked the large wooden entrance door leading onto the towpath. One evening after completing this routine and confident that all visitors had left, he retired to the staff room in the office block, locked the entrance door behind him and began to prepare his supper before carrying out his security rounds. Unfortunately, a family was still in the yard, and after shouting in vain to attract attention, they used a crowbar to force an exit. The lock held but the upper hinge of the very large door fractured, allowing it to fall inwards and providing a means of escape. It was a happy ending for them, but imagine the problem it presented our security man when he tried to lock up after completing his duties!

Almost before the ship arrived in Bristol, members of the public had been offering artifacts and documents more or less relevant to it, or at least to nineteenth-century maritime history. At first it was thought that some of these might be displayed on board, but it was quickly realised that it would be many years before secure and weatherproof space could be provided. When the ship docked, a small lean-to room below the office had been equipped as a first aid post, and for the first few weeks it was manned by members of St John Ambulance. Happily, there was virtually no demand for this service, so the space was converted into our first dockside museum. Rather to our surprise, the flow of potential exhibits continued in succeeding years, and we gradually expanded our display area. First we used a small, disused workshop behind the lean-to, and later a small area of the main warehouse beside the office entrance. Except for the heating and lighting, all the alterations and decorations were carried out by our exhibition staff during winter. Show cases were adapted from redundant shop fittings given us by friendly businessmen, and from the racks of storage bins fitted in the small workshop. During those early years the restoration of the ship demanded every penny of our income, so we could not afford professional help in setting out such displays. But we were fortunate to receive plenty of friendly advice from the professionals, and in the end we achieved a layout that presented a logical historical sequence. Our amateur efforts were certainly rewarded by the public's interest in the museum; even in winter it was rare not to find someone browsing quietly through the rather chilly rooms.

As soon as it had been decided to open the ship every day I set out to find a system of staffing which could operate without introducing endless overtime and imposing unnecessary stress on our small team. It seemed that a shift system akin to the one used on board ships in harbour might be appropriate, so the small staff was split into three groups of two or three members, each group working for four days followed by two days off. Thus we always had two-thirds of our employees on duty, and in an emergency we could bring the others in by paying overtime. One person in each group was designated the security man, responsible for the opening and closing routines.

By adjusting working hours, groups alternated between early shifts and late, so all took a turn in opening and closing. With such a small staff flexibility had to be the keynote, and all members were expected to take turns in the pay box and shop. Guides for parties were provided by volunteers from the staff or by the management and security during opening hours devolved on all of us; we were certainly not troubled by idleness.

Management also presented a

The author (left) with Tim Webb on the visitor's temporary walkway.
(Photograph: Bath and West Evening Chronicle)

problem because at the beginning either the commercial manager, Tim Webb, or I had to be in attendance whenever the ship was open, to supervise and to be responsible for the takings. We adopted a five-day week which covered Saturdays and Sundays, and it was many years before I was again to have a free weekend.

To complete our management team came office manager Ken Moody and secretary Joan Andrews, working a normal five-day week. Apart from keeping the books of both the project and the trading company, Ken maintained the numerous records essential for the proper supervision of a cash business. A great deal of Joan's time was spent in answering the tele-phone, and she quickly developed the public relation approach essential to our type of activity. She also established a system of booking parties which survived substantially unchanged almost to the present day.

So from that original desk and chair evolved an effective management structure and a cheerful, willing team determined to make a success of our enterprise. Even after the first year there were still some in Bristol who predicted our eventual failure, but they succeeded only in stiffening our resolve to disprove them. Above all, we were determined to show that the *Great Britain* would never become a charge on the Bristol ratepayers.

7—How We Managed

When a ship enters a repair yard for a refit its owners normally prepare a specification listing all the work to be undertaken. So long as sufficient detail is given, the shipyard can provide an estimate of cost to be agreed between the parties before work begins. During the refit a representative of the owners, sometimes known as a marine superintendent, attends at the yard to check and approve work in progress and to agree any amendments or supplementary items.

In the case of the s.s. *Great Britain*, Dr Corlett had prepared the owners' specification for restoration and repair. But because of the state of the ship and the unique nature of the task, it was obvious that the repairers, Charles Hill, would need us frequently to amplify instructions. I soon found that my position was akin to that of a marine superintendent, but although I was capable of monitoring work in progress, I at first lacked the detailed knowledge of the ship that was needed to handle the yard's queries.

I had assumed that Dr Corlett would pay regular visits, but it soon became apparent that his professional life was so demanding that he would not have the time to attend to every detail of the work. An attempt was made to resolve the complex question of repairs to the crack in the starboard side by holding a meeting with the repairers, but after lengthy discussions it was clear to me that many questions remained unresolved. There was nothing else for it; I would have to study the details of the restoration programme so that I could act as an effective link between our naval architect and the shipyard.

I had understood from my first sight of the vessel the enormity of the task that lay ahead. In normal circumstances any shipyard would have classified the ship as 'beyond economical repair' and recommended that it should go for scrap, and Charles Hill faced a daunting undertaking, with no prior experience to assist them. Because of the state of the hull and the many major structural repairs and alterations, it seemed to me apt to divide the restoration work into two main phases, the rebuilding of the hull and the fitting out of the vessel.

The first logical action in restoring such a hull for service would have been to scale and clean it inside and out, and then replace all deficient plates and sections. But this was no ordinary hull; it was the first ocean-going iron hull in the world, whose every single piece, down to the humble rivet, had a story to tell. Our techniques had to aim for the maximum degree of preservation of the original, and the minimum of replacement to maintain adequate overall strength. Our early plans also centred on the importance of replacing the weather deck, so that the interior of the vessel could dry out. Such factors affecting priorities and procedures meant that instead of giving the shipyard a free hand, the order of doing things had to be controlled by the project.

31

Dr Corlett's restoration specification had now to become the basis of a work schedule in which progress depended on the availability of funds. My experience of project management in the Ministry of Defence suggested that the large project committee, shortly to become the project council, could not be responsible for detailed restoration policy, so I suggested that a small technical management committee should be established to decide the ongoing work programme, approve designs and procedures and inspect work in progress. The result was the ship committee, originally known as the dock committee, which held its first meeting in Bristol in November 1970. Membership initially consisted of Dr Corlett as chairman, Richard Goold-Adams who, as chairman of the project, could authorise expenditure, Jim Goodier, the senior Lloyds surveyor in Bristol and myself as secretary. We were most fortunate that Lloyds Register of Shipping had offered professional advice free of charge, a gesture that has given us the benefit of a senior surveyor on our ship committee right down to the present day.

Again using my service experience, I drafted the minutes of meetings both to provide a record of restoration progress and prescribe any action to be carried out.

Generally speaking, the initiation of new or continuing work on the ship was my responsibility, and I became the executive officer carrying out the instructions of the ship committee. In this way I gradually assumed the responsibility for drafting specifications and instructions for contractors, including the preparation of drawings by our part-time draughtsman at the dock. Of course, when any work involved important structural alterations or repairs, the drawings were invariably referred to our naval architect for professional assessment and approval.

In the early days, when most of the work could be described as structural first aid and preservation, financial management consisted of authorising expenditure as funds became available. There were frequent periods of several months when work virtually came to a halt for lack of money, periods of frustration during which we explored every possibility of making some progress. The subject of bringing in voluntary workers was often discussed, but this could not be done without the agreement of the shipbuilding trades unions, who had the power to black work on our ship. In several meetings we tried to persuade the unions that our ship might be seen as a museum exhibit akin to a steam locomotive, rather than just another ship to be repaired. They did not share this view, but they finally agreed that voluntary workers could be used so long as they had the appropriate craft skills and were fully paid-up members of the relevant trades union. Perhaps not surprisingly, none of our local supporters met such demanding criteria.

We also tried to win union agreement for our own staff to do unskilled work on board the ship, but this was also vetoed. At last, in 1976, it was agreed that we could engage a seaman recently retired from the Falkland Islands as ship keeper; his permitted range of duties was strictly limited, but his role was eventually accepted by the shipyard shop stewards.

Throughout the first two years

32

the head office of the project was in London premises provided rent-free by friends in the business world, at first in Chancery Lane and later in Cannon Street. Then, in the autumn of 1972, came a dramatic change; the chairman telephoned me to say we had been asked to evacuate the London office, and it had been decided to accommodate the general secretary in the dockside premises in Bristol—within weeks! Fortunately, we had a large drawing office that housed our part-time draughtsman and served as a room for meetings, and by partitioning off about a third of it we created an office big enough for him and his personal secretary. The reduced drawing office was still ample for our meetings and to house the draughtsman.

By the time the office files and equipment arrived from London in October we had brought in second-hand furniture and arranged for alterations to our telephone system. So it was with great disappointment that we learned that our popular general secretary had decided to leave his post and not move to Bristol; after all our efforts, our splendid new office at first housed nothing more exciting than piles of files and records.

Partly because of our financial position and partly because of the uncertainty of the ship's future in Bristol, the post of general secretary remained temporarily unfilled and I found myself performing this extra role, ably assisted by our office secretary, who somehow coped with the additional paperwork.

Together we reorganised the ex-London files and drew up a combined filing system for the Bristol office. By then our project had become a company limited by guar-antee, with the general secretary nominated as company secretary. Our commercial manager Tim Webb nobly assumed this office as a temporary measure, but it was several years before we had in Robin Bradbury a general secretary once again carrying out the full duties of the post. In the meantime various people were appointed to carry out the fund-raising task in either a full- or part-time capacity, and this at least eased my administrative burden.

Once defined restoration work began it became possible to introduce a form of budgetary control, with an annual programme of expenditure presented to the project council for approval. This was based on conservative estimates of income, although there was some flexibility to allow for both unforeseen expenses and unexpected windfalls. Only once did we consider borrowing from the bank, when our weather deck was being relaid and some £30,000 was needed to avoid interrupting the work half way through. Scarcely had I approached our banker when a totally unexpected windfall of well over £30,000 arrived in the form of a legacy from a recently deceased supporter!

Throughout the first few years we were constantly bedevilled by uncertainties stemming from the insecurity of our Bristol site. There were threats that the ship would have to move elsewhere in the City Docks, plans to move her to London, Portsmouth and even Plymouth, and opponents who forecast an early death for the project. My policy was to leave all these matters to the project council and to concentrate every effort on the success of our enterprise, never doubting that the *Great Britain* was in Bristol to stay.

8—The Benefits of Begging

Charity had saved the *Great Britain* from a watery grave in the Falklands, and it quickly became clear that only charity could now save her from the scrapyard. Government money was not available for projects such as ours, and an application to the local authority led nowhere. There is no doubt that the live visual impact of the decayed and rusting hull was a shock to many who had perhaps gained a false impression from television.

Our general secretary, as now, carried the heavy responsibility of fund-raising, but if we were to succeed, every supporter had to be ready to exploit any offer of materials or money. I had had no previous experience of the art of begging, but I quickly began to learn the rules. I discovered , for instance, that large business firms are constantly improving their office facilities and often have surplus furniture for disposal.

Naturally, the obvious material needs of our well publicised restoration plans raised the hopes of hordes of company salesmen, who began calling in considerable numbers. I determined to demonstrate that we were a businesslike organisation, but would expect to be offered charitable terms. After a representative had spent a little time extolling his wares, it was my usual practice to explain that the project was a charity; how much of the product would his company be prepared to donate, and what special terms might be offered for subsequent purchases? Not only did

this approach quickly dispose of a substantial percentage of the travellers, but it did indeed clinch the donation of a considerable quantity of materials and services, together with handsome discounts on later supplies.

As for manufacturing to our special requirements, firms have been able to help in two basic ways. Because we were not working to a deadline, some were able to slot our products into gaps in normal production. We had to provide drawings and specifications and sometimes materials, but the actual manufacture was often free of charge. Other companies were able to produce items using apprentice labour, which provided both training and the interest of an involvement in our project.

Through members of our project council and as a result of visits to the ship, many senior executives have taken a keen interest in the restoration. In a book such as this it would be impossible to list all our commercial benefactors, but suffice it to say that they range from the largest public companies to small private firms. For example, one company presented us with a new funnel constructed to our drawings and delivered to the dock, while a small firm manufactured all the brass gratings for the deck scuppers. For many years a supplier of industrial clothing has met all the needs of our maintenance staff and volunteers entirely free of charge.

There are inevitable disadvantages in accepting offers of goods and services on a charitable basis. In general, when the firm plans to fit our job into an anticipated slack period delivery is agreed accordingly, but if there is a sudden upsurge in business we take second place. In these circumstances progress chasing must take the form of tactful letters or telephone calls rather than peremptory telex messages! Some firms like to publicise their involvement with the project, and time has then to be given to helping their public relations people to prepare articles and photographs for trade publications or advertisements.

Acknowledgements of practical assistance consist of the inclusion of the company's name on a list posted at the dock—and in the case of substantial help, the election of the company to honorary membership of the project. The latter provides continuing association through newsletters, and a membership certificate that can be framed and displayed on the firm's premises.

Within a remarkably short time we had received innumerable offers of help from firms, colleges, other establishments and individuals, only a few of which had an immediate application. I set up a filing system to ensure that contact could be regained and an offer taken up at the appropriate time, and by this method we kept in touch with many good friends who have helped us regularly over the years.

Although I am happy to say that raising money has not been my direct concern, donations have made an essential contribution to the success of the project. At an early stage, individuals were welcomed as members in exchange for either a lump sum gift or a covenanted subscription; later we also offered a less formal association as a friend of the project for a modest annual contribution, but as inflation hit in the 1970's and our restoration costs soared, our cash income seemed pitifully small.

Then came a new turning point in 1983, when Prince Andrew, now the Duke of York, agreed to become our patron. Almost simultaneously the BBC offered us the opportunity to make a five-minute appeal on television, and we were delighted when our new young patron agreed to present it himself. After the broadcast, donations came in at a steady rate until we received a phone call from a firm of accountants in London to say that an important client had seen it, and might agree to make a substantial contribution. Within days we had received £60,000 from J. Paul Getty Junior, who also expressed an interest in continuing his support. He has been as good as his word, and further donations from him and from our founder benefactor, Sir Jack Hayward, have ensured that the restoration programme has been able to keep up the kind of momentum to offer some prospect of its reaching its planned conclusion.

In spite of this transformation of our finances, it would be impossible to over-estimate the benefits the project has gained through the years from gifts of materials and practical assistance. In the early days they probably made the difference between success and failure; the unfailing support and generosity of so many friends in industry was certainly a boost to my morale, and helped to reassure me when the going was rough.

9—We Become a Shipyard

By the end of 1971 the relationship between Charles Hill and Sons and the project had fallen into a routine pattern. The restoration work approved by the ship committee was passed to the yard in the form of written instructions, together with any necessary supporting drawings. If an outside contractor was involved we normally negotiated terms direct, but Charles Hill provided such supporting services as scaffolding, electric power and so on.

With some specific jobs a price was quoted, otherwise a daily labour charge was agreed. Charles Hill's repairs manager supervised the work, while I checked and accepted it on behalf of the project, and when an account was received I verified it before passing it to the chairman.

This cosy arrangement came to an abrupt end in 1977, when Charles Hill and Sons' Bristol shipyard was closed in line with the city council's policy to phase out commercial shipping activities in the city docks. The nearest firm specialising in ship repair was now Jefferies of Avonmouth, a member of the Charles Hill group with which we had had previous contact. The yard and the Great Western Dock in which the *Great Britain* sat had up to now been rented by Charles Hill from its owner, Bristol City Council, and it was now proposed that the tenancy should be transferred to our project. Since we had by then demonstrated the seriousness and viability of our plans, the council generously agreed to grant us a lease of the dock at a peppercorn rent.

That, at least, was good news, but it did mean that my responsibilities would grow considerably, since in effect I would become the manager of a small dockyard. This position carries all the legal responsibilities of a dockmaster. Over and above this, not only were we to lose the services of our main contractor, but suddenly we were responsible for the maintenance of the premises, the dry dock and its associated machinery, the provision of scaffolding and dockyard services, and above all, for safety in all its aspects.

As we approached our 'big bang' Charles Hill was busy disposing of shipyard equipment, and there was concern that our dock might be denuded. Fortunately, the company's management continued its benevolent attitude towards us, with the result that we were given all the plant associated with our dock except the crane, for which we paid a very modest charge, and the scaffolding around the ship.

At this time we still had only our one shipkeeper on ship maintenance, and the immediate need was for a crane driver. A director of Charles Hill gave me the names of two of their drivers who had just been made redundant, and while one had decided to emigrate to Australia the other, by happy chance a regular driver of our crane, accepted my offer of employment.

To recap, the Great Western

Dock was excavated in the 1830's and much of the stonework is original. The dock gate or caisson dates from 1928, and most of the machinery, including the pump, had been in use for many years. The supervision and maintenance of all this placed a considerable extra burden on me, and it was partly in recognition of this that my title was changed to project director. My colleague the commercial manager virtually took over the supervision of the exhibition side, becoming, in effect, the managing director of the trading company.

The greatest change was in running the restoration programme. All our contractors now had to come in from outside and at first, since few had much knowledge of ship repair, I had to give them more detailed instructions and carry out the supervisory role of repairs manager. At that time we were making plans to begin the task of replanking the entire weather deck apart from the forecastle, which Charles Hill had completed some years earlier. One or two local firms expressed an interest in tendering for this task, but most lacked the specialised woodworking skills of the ancient craft of shipwright.

Then befell the sort of stroke of good fortune that posterity sees as a turning point. The last foreman of shipwrights of Charles Hill and Son, a man, of course, well known to me, was a member of a family that had lived in the little riverside port of Pill for many years. With the shakeup he and a son who was also a qualified shipwright set up the ship repairing business of D.J.Williams (Shipwrights) Ltd. Shortly afterwards he called on me and expressed an interest in contracting for work, and when he submitted a tender for the decklaying it emerged as by far the lowest we had received.

At the next meeting of the ship committee there was some anxiety about placing such an important contract with a newly established firm, but it was agreed that it was worth the risk to gain the services of skilled craftsmen. So began a relationship between the project and D.J.Williams that has continued to the time of writing. By increasing and diversifying his work force he has been able to meet almost all our demands, greatly reducing the need for other contractors and simplifying our management task.

From small beginnings we gradually built up our maintenance team until the time came when I felt the need for some managerial assistance. This led to the creation of a post we first called the project bosun but later, when the engine installation was imminent, the project engineer. We had come a long way from the day when I began with one desk and a telephone.

10—Demon Decay

It is hard to find words to describe the extremities of deterioration and decay in almost every corner of the vessel before we started work, yet beneath it all there remained an innate strength demonstrated by the ship's amazing survival both of years of neglect and of the stresses and strains of the salvage operation.

The planking of the weather deck was riddled with wet rot, making those early walkways a vital necessity. Most of the interior decking had been removed in the Falkland Islands, but enough sound planking remained in the forecastle to make restoration possible. The heavy timbers of the bulwarks and even of the wood keel added in 1852 presented a sorry sight, but on closer inspection we were able to save and restore a substantial amount of them.

We all know about rusting, the oxidation of iron to form reddish dust of iron oxide. When moisture and oxygen abound this process continues relentlessly until all the steel is eaten away on, say, the door of a car, but happily the *Great Britain* fared better than this. Of course, its plating was much thicker than the skin of a car, but the real answer lay in its metallic qualities, for it was wrought iron, and not steel. Unarguably modern steel, which was not available in 1840, is superior to wrought iron as a shipbuilding material, but wrought iron behaves in a different way when exposed to the effects of corrosion. Instead of powdery rust, a hard, impermeable substance called scale forms on its surface, acting almost like a protective skin. There is inevitably some penetration by moisture and air to create a degree of rusting, but the process is slowed dramatically, and a neglected iron structure will tend to survive far longer than a steel one.

During his survey of the ship in the Falkland Islands Dr. Corlett was able to measure the thickness of several areas of the hull plating, and found the wastage of the lower parts surprisingly small. In fact areas above the waterline that had experienced the effects of wind, water and temperature variations had suffered far more severely, and here many plates were holed. Nevertheless, the ship's frames and beams still provided such collective strength that the hull form remained almost perfect, in spite of local weaknesses like that famous crack in the starboard side. I saw this at first hand when I instructed Charles Hill to replace a length of beam, at the lower 'tween level, that had been cut out at least 50 years before. To the amazement of the workmen, the piece fitted exactly between the two lengths still connected to the hull to port and starboard, proof positive that there had been no deformation or 'bagging' of the hull plating, in spite of the crack. This and other experiences bolstered my confidence in the ship, but from my first visit aboard I never doubted the feasibility of the restoration.

Although it did not provide a safe walking surface, the decayed

The forecastle deck before restoration, and below, the bottom plating before de-scaling.

weather deck did offer the interior some protection against the worst of the weather, and it was decided to leave it virtually undisturbed and concentrate first on cleaning and preserving the ironwork. The ship's structure and plating are held together by rivets which tend to loosen through stresses and strains on a ship and corrosion, so we chose a cleaning method that avoided, as far as possible, the shock of such standard equipment as pneumatic scaling hammers. The ship committee settled for the comparatively modern technique of high-pressure water cleaning, capable of removing even the heaviest scale deposits. In one area of the lower hull pieces of scale as big as dinner plates and nearly an inch thick were blown off the sound plating beneath. For this type of operation specially trained workers are essential, so before work could begin we had to seek the agreement of the shipyard unions to the introduction of an outside contractor. This was negotiated on the understanding that the shipyard workers provided all the supporting services and the painters would coat the structure after cleaning, and it caused some problems. With this type of task the rate of progress inevitably varies, and it was not economic to employ a continuous support group from the shipyard. Clashes in priority between our contract and other shipyard work meant that sometimes the cleaning contractor was waiting for scaffolding, or areas of freshly cleaned iron were rusting for lack of a prompt coat of red lead.

An issue that received much early attention was the decision to remove the timber cladding from the hull. Added in 1882 when the ship was converted to carry cargo, it consisted of pitch pine planking laid lengthways on the ship's side plating and bolted in place by 7/8 inch bolts. It extended from a line roughly three feet below the original passenger ship waterline up to a point above the new deep-laden cargo waterline, and seams were caulked so that the area provided an outer hull to stiffen the parts of the side plating not designed to take continuous water pressure. I can only surmise that this cladding offered a cheaper option than the alternative of replating much of the hull.

The planking was secured by about 10,000 bolts of varying lengths, some passing through the plating only, others through plating, frames and the occasional bracket for other pieces of internal structure. It was clear from the start that its removal would not only turn the ship into a pepper pot, but also possibly cause a degree of weakening of the structural integrity of the original hull. A few pessimists even suggested that the iron plates behind the cladding might prove to be so badly corroded that the removal of the support and protection of the timber would be disastrous, but if we were to return the ship to its 1843 appearance the cladding had to come off. For example, almost all the original porthole positions were hidden behind it.

To seal the bolt holes and reduce any possible weakening of the hull we ordered bolts with heads shaped to give the appearance of rivets. These were manufactured by a friendly company which supplied them as a donation. Charles Hill and Sons were given the contract and the tedious task began, for though a surprising number of the original nuts could be unscrewed and the bolts punched out, many

Top: Cleaning and de-scaling plating using high pressure water.

Bottom: Applying patches of glass reinforced plastic to decayed areas of plating.

planks had to be forced off or split with wedges. As the original iron hull emerged to view after some 90 years we were relieved to find it in fair condition, and no apparent damage or deformation was detected. After the new bolts had been inserted and the water blasters had cleaned the surface the hull plating looked in altogether better shape, apart from the occasional jagged hole caused by corrosion. Our decision to remove the cladding had certainly been vindicated though it created the unforeseen problem of providing storage and a future use for a vast stock of pitch-pine planking!

An indirect benefit of the water blasting was that it gave an idea of the strength of the surviving structure. An area of plate that has successfully withstood pressures of 10,000 lb per square inch can reasonably be regarded as fit for many more years of life. But there were numerous areas of weakness, including those holed plates, and we had to plan our strategy carefully. After detailed survey it was agreed that the collective strength of the hull was more than adequate to survive in the dock for very many years, and that the wholesale renewal of the thinner plates would not be necessary. Instead we plumped for a patching technique using glass-reinforced plastic, in which weak or holed plates were sandwiched between layers of GRP bonded to them; this restored watertightness and added a measure of strength to the structure. Another advantage was that the lines of rivets and the fascinating hand-crafted butt straps did not have to be disturbed. Where the GRP overlaid them their shape showed through, so that the skills of the early iron workers were preserved to maximum effect.

On arrival in Bristol the hold deck, or tank top as it is technically known, had remained virtually untouched since the water had been pumped out in Sparrow Cove. It presented an almost indescribable scene of dereliction, its floor a sea of mud interspersed with coils of wire and other debris and the pillars hanging with corrosion and decaying marine life. It was thought likely that much material related to the ship might be lying hidden beneath the mud, and the task of clearance almost took the form of an archaeological dig. Our efforts were rewarded by the discovery of items that included an original Trotman anchor and two lead lavatory pans, one of which retained much of its decorated ceramic lining.

Beneath the tank tops, in effect an early form of double bottom, the spaces were mostly filled with mud and scale, and their clearance posed formidable problems. Some manholes were accessible only to extremely small people, and it is conceivable that these spaces were intended to be cleaned by boys employed in shipyards in the early nineteenth century.

As we lifted the covers from the tank spaces aft we had a surprise; these were the original freshwater tanks of the ship and still contained a substantial amount of pure water, undisturbed for at least 35 years.

Since then, steady progress has been made in the task of reversing and controlling the forces of decay. Like any other ship, the *Great Britain* lies in the open, exposed to the elements, so the battle against corrosion will never end. Of course the ideal solution would be to house the entire vessel in an enormous building with a controlled environment, but in the absence of that ideal we must continue to exploit every new development of techniques and materials to uphold our fight against demon decay.

The funnel transforms the ship's appearance.

11—The Phoenix Rises

The depressing and expensive task of cleaning and preserving the hull seemed to stretch endlessly into the future, and even the laborious peeling of the cladding timbers from the ship's side scarcely indicated progress to any but the discerning eye. What we needed was a concentrated effort to transform a small and specific part of the ship, something that would raise our morale and show everyone we meant business. The forecastle virtually suggested itself, not only because it was an area most urgently in need of repair but because it had defined limits. Perhaps best of all, in the long run, its restoration would immediately be visible to the people of Bristol.

At first there were high hopes that a new weather deck would be laid on the forecastle in a matter of months, but it soon became clear that much preparatory work would have to be completed first. In 1857 the original flush-decked forecastle was stepped, with its forward part raised above the original level. At the same time the deck openings were modified, and even the position of the crew's W.C.'s, the 'heads', had to be changed. Another major alteration was to the position of the hawsepipes, which were placed at a much higher level with their tubes passing through the upper level of the forecastle, including the original 'heads'. From the evidence of the interior we were confident that the original hawsepipes remained in place and had simply been blanked off externally, but the removal of the later pair presented a formi-

dable problem. They were so firmly built into the bows that their removal seemed likely to result in damage that could lead to a major and expensive degree of reconstruction. Reluctantly, we decided that the upper pipes would not be disturbed; the cost is that our visitors must forever be informed why the ship has two pairs of hawsepipes!

It now remained to check and restore the weather deck beams of the forecastle. Many were in good condition, but new ones had to be installed at the forward end to complete the original flush deck. The cropped outboard ends of these beams were easily identified, so their replacements could be precisely located. Provision was made for the three entrances at the after end of the deck to give access to the officers', petty officers' and crew's quarters, but because of the upper hawsepipes the restoration of the original crew's 'heads' was not possible. Instead the two entrances were restored in the form of dummy companionway hatch covers to be screwed to the deck after it had been laid.

Running fore and aft on the centreline, supporting the deck beams at each level of the forecastle, were heavy timber carlins between which were several timber pillars. It was found to be possible to preserve most of this timberwork except for the carlin at the weather deck level, but some of the timber pillars were very weak, and the forecastle was therefore stiffened by installing two steel pillars from top to bottom on the centreline, connecting to the carlins at each deck level.

As built in 1843, the foremast was stepped at the break of the forecastle with a hinged socket just above the level of the main deck. Below the deck a heavy timber spar carried the mast load down to the keel within the forecastle, evidence of which remained in the form of wooden mast partners. This lower spar was renewed by installing a steel tube of the same diameter, and this later carried the load of the new foremast. Before this a steel framework had been built close abaft the decayed forecastle bulkhead in order to stiffen the vessel, and it was now found to be possible to connect it to the mast tube. It meant the latter was supported independently of the fragile wooden partners, and together with the bulkhead stiffener it formed a strong tripod-like construction.

Throughout those early years our project council was constantly concerned about the continued exposure of the ship's interior to the elements. It was even suggested that a form of temporary cover should be improvised, but this would have been expensive and would have impeded the flow of visitors. Instead there was renewed determination to speed up our preparations for deck laying, which gradually took precedence over other work.

Even before the completion of our pilot scheme the pressure was on to begin preparations for laying the main deck. But compared with the forecastle these were considerably more complex and extensive, in that we had to convert the 1882 deck layout of the sailing cargo ship into that of the original passenger liner. For example, in 1843 there was only one small cargo hatchway, which still existed just aft of the foremast. In 1882 came an additional three large cargo hatches with deep iron coamings standing proud of the deck level.

The priority task was to prepare and install all the structural features that had to be in place at the weather deck level before any planks could be laid. Essentially, these were the funnel, the partner for the mainmast and heavy metal shoes to receive the hinged sockets of the four masts abaft the bridge. Spurred by offers from manufacturers to donate these items, we hastened to prepare for their installation.

The addition of the funnel, standing 38 feet above the deck and eight feet in diameter, at once transformed the appearance of the vessel and gave a clear signal that we meant business. Constructed of small curved plates riveted together, it must look very similar to its iron predecessor, but its method of installation was very different. When the engine and boilers were removed in 1882 the whole machinery space was converted into a cargo hold, access to which was provided by a hatchway built into the opening in the deck for the funnel uptake. Our task was to reverse this procedure, and it was found to be possible to embody part of the hatch coaming in the reproduction of the funnel skirt. As there were no plans to instal a boiler, the funnel was designed as a dummy, with a steel 'lid' to keep the rain out. It was mounted on a circular steel plate supported in the centre of the hatchway, with steel pillars beneath to carry the extra load down to the keel. The total weight of the funnel was more than seven tons, so it had to be built in three sections capable of being lifted by the dock's three-ton derrick. A feature of the funnel is the circular jacket tank around its base, which originally contained the boiler feedwater. Because of the low pressure of the steam, water from this tank, pre-heated by the funnel gases, could be fed into the boilers by gravity. An essential part of this system was a pipe from the top of the tank leading up the funnel and open to atmospheric pressure. It was the accidental sealing of one of these pipes in the P and S.S. *Great Eastern* that led to the explosion that marred her trial voyage and hastened the death of Brunel.

Amid all the trials and tribulations there were even some critics who asserted that our *Great Britain* was not the original! Apart from the exactitude of the dimensions there remained the indisputable evidence of the registered number carved into the structure of the central cargo hatch, and we were relieved, to say the least, to find that this agreed with the original registration in Bristol. Now we were about to alter the cargo hatch, and had to ensure the continuity of that all-important number. Carefully selecting an area of original structure which we knew would never be disturbed, we arranged for it to be re-carved and formally certified by our Lloyds surveyor, before the part of the hatchway bearing the original number was cut away in readiness to receive the funnel.

Another major external feature restored at this stage was the flying bridge, a simple timber platform spanning the ship immediately behind the funnel. Ocean-going paddle steamers seem to have been fitted with a bridge or catwalk between the paddle boxes, and it has been suggested that its main use was in rough weather, when frequent engine orders were required as the paddles lifted from the sea or dug deeply as the vessel rolled. This problem does not arise in a screw-driven ship, and it is possible that the *Great Britain's* bridge was part of her original design as a paddle steamer. No doubt the deck officers discovered the advantage of an elevated platform clear of passengers and other distractions.

The replacement bridge has been constructed in close conformity with the original, using heavy timber beams of pitch pine supporting a classic wooden grating deck. The top of the small deckhouse abaft the funnel, originally the access to the engine room, forms the centre of the bridge, with its two timber wings extending out to port and starboard. These are supported at their outer ends by braced iron pillars based on the gunwale; because of local weaknesses in the latter, short lengths of it were rebuilt in steel abreast the bridge to ensure that the weight of the wings could be borne safely.

The final major task to be accomplished before the deck laying was the repair of the crack. Soon after the ship's return to Bristol the entrance above it had been adapted to receive a passenger gangway from the dockside, as early visitors may recall. During salvage operations heavy steel plates had been laid across and fastened to the deck beams at both the weather deck and upper 'tween deck levels, and obviously the topmost salvage strap had to be removed before any deck planks could be laid. A decision on the repair of the crack could no longer be delayed.

When the opening for wool bales had been cut in the Falklands, a

The flying bridge built in timber as the original. (Photograph: Colin Momber, P.B.A.)

length of the sheer strake, the topmost band of plates, had been removed, and several deck beams foreshortened. A careful check of the structure revealed that, in spite of the crack and the stresses im-

The vertical crack in the starboard side awaiting repair.

posed on the hull during the salvage, there was no major misalignment of the ship's side, and the replacement of the strake should present no problem. Repairs went ahead accordingly, until at last the salvage engineer's strap was lifted from the ship, leaving a fair line of restored deck beams ready for planking. On the deck below it was found to be possible to leave the salvage strap undisturbed as part of the entrance decking. As there seemed no reason to remove the extra stiffening installed at the lower levels, this remains as evidence of the problems presented by the crack during the salvage. Fortunately, by this time Bristol City Council had agreed that the ship would not have to move from the Great Western Dock, so it was no longer necessary to ensure that the restored hull would be capable of floating. Set against this, because of

an ever-present threat that a failure of the stop gates at Cumberland Basin could lead to a major rise in the harbour water level, we had to be prepared for the possibility of our dry dock becoming flooded. In these circumstances it could be disastrous if the ship lifted off its blocks, so we have had to arrange that if the worst came to the worst the hull would flood and keep the vessel anchored. One outcome is that it has not been necessary to carry out a seagoing repair to the crack below the water line; instead we have applied our routine patching procedure using glass-reinforced plastic.

So at last sufficient preparatory structural work had been completed for a start to be made with the deck-laying. Many minor changes remained to be made, but we elected to carry these out piecemeal as planking went ahead.

12—A Weather Deck At Last

Even before the ship arrived in Bristol, the project had negotiated the purchase of some 40,000 feet of second-hand pitch pine planking which had floored parts of the Royal Naval Barracks at Portsmouth since the turn of the century. To create a shipboard atmosphere the Board of Admiralty had decreed that the floors were to be laid like a deck, properly caulked and seamed and secured down by coach screws from beneath. As a result this material promised to be ideal for our purposes, although the plank thickness, which averaged less than $2^{1}/_{2}$ inches, was barely adequate as a replacement for the original three-inch red pine planks. Nevertheless, enough of it to deck the forecastle was selected in 1973.

Most of the planks contained old coach screws, numerous small nails and the residue of caulking materials, all of which had to be removed carefully before a local sawmill would accept them for planing to a uniform thickness and for cutting a caulking rebate. After one or two metallic objects had damaged the planing blade we had to arrange for every plank to pass over a metal detector to locate buried nails.

It is well known that decks caulked in the traditional way with oakum and pitch need constant maintenance to keep them watertight. To overcome this, a modern method using polysulphide rubber has been developed, and the prospect of keeping down maintenance costs prompted us to adopt it for the new decking of the *Great Britain*.

Theoretically this elastic material bonds to the wood on each side of the seam, to maintain a watertight seal however much the timber moves through expansion and contraction. In practice the results are sometimes disappointing and the *Great Britain*, along with some other vessels using this new system, has experienced the annoyance of a leaking deck.

At last in 1974 came the great day when the first plank of the forecastle deck was laid. We had noted that the surviving planks at the second level were laid diagonally from the centreline, and a careful examination of the holes in the original weather deck beams revealed that the same had applied there. We concluded that the planking had been laid in this way to help counteract the twisting strains on the bow of the ship at sea, no doubt an example of Brunel's use of timber as part of a structural whole.

As with most ships of the period, the deck of the *Great Britain* was drained by simple lead scuppers in the form of ducts through the side, ending in a spout. Because of the tumble home, (the way the sides of some ships incline inwards above their extreme breadths), these discharges inevitably ran down the plating, creating areas of heavy local corrosion. In the interests of preservation we adopted a recessed scupper which would fit neatly into the gutterways and convey water to the dock bottom via a system of pipes hidden in the hull. At the same time, most of the original lead

49

The forecastle deck completed, but only a small part of the total decklaying task.

The circular skylight arrives before the deck beams are ready.

scuppers were restored *in situ* to preserve the evidence of the earlier system.

The successful completion of the forecastle simply served to emphasise what a small proportion of the vessel's deck area had been covered, and pressure mounted to complete the preparations to tackle the main deck. At a length of 270 feet the cost was prohibitive, but there were obvious advantages in treating the task as a continuing evolution. By 1976 the flow of visitors was increasing each year and our income from subscribers also showed an upward trend, so it was likely that we could meet the cost so long as the work extended over three successive financial years. The die was cast, and the deck laying contract began in 1977.

Apart from its self-evident function of providing both a walking surface and a watertight cover, the deck of a ship forms part of the structural whole. The beams beneath the planks both support the deck and provide athwartships strength, but the planks collectively act like a girder, giving the ship important longitudinal stiffness. Because of the extensive overhang of the counter at the stern the need for the strengthening effect of a deck was regarded as urgent, and that is why the laying programme was begun from aft.

Although the major structural preparations had been completed, plenty of other details remained to be dealt with in advance of the planking. Looking ahead, I realised that the tailshaft, which would eventually carry the weight of the propeller, had to be placed in the after hold before the after cargo hatch was decked over. Fortunately, we quickly found a donor willing to make this essential feature in time to avoid delaying the decking programme.

The state of the gunwale was a particular headache, and at first it seemed likely to delay progress. There was early optimism that most of the heavy timbers would respond to the ministrations of a specialist timber treatment company, but as the work progressed it became evident that at least half were beyond saving. Most of the bulwark timber at the forward end was restored successfully, but substantial lengths of the gunwale abaft the bridge to port and starboard had to be wholly or partially replaced. For the capping across the top of the transom replacement in heavy timber sections was the only possible option, but the total replacement of the main gunwales in timber presented the dual problem of obtaining the lengths of section required and of meeting the considerable cost of them. The possibility of rebuilding lengths in steel, as we had done below the bridge, was considered and rejected in favour of moulding them in reinforced cement. As a result we ended up with a complete gunwale with lengths variously constructed of restored wood, new wood, steel plate and cement, but in spite of the apparent incompatibility of these materials, we are left with a realistic border to the weather deck that does not demand any exceptional maintenance attention. Before deck laying began all the timber structures to be built into it had been designed, and the two companionway hatch covers on the quarters, later to give access to the promenade saloon below, had been installed. Also with us at the dock were the total of 18 rectangular skylights, and one circular one.

Since the deck was to be laid in three stages, preparations were first concentrated on the after third of the total length. All the surviving iron deck beams were examined carefully and repaired as necessary before being cleaned and painted; some were renewed in steel, and several needed adjustment to achieve a fair line for the planking. The heavy coaming of the after cargo hatch was cut down flush with the beams, but instead of disturbing its lower frame, new lengths of beam were installed across it. The 1882 after companionway on the centreline was similarly dealt with, while two new deck openings were established to provide access for the forward companionways as fitted in 1843, between the after promenade saloon and the weather deck.

The earlier removal of the rotted deck planks had revealed that part of the circle of angle iron that supported the original circular skylight remained in position, but the site for the skylight partially overlapped the later structure of the 1857 lifting propeller trunk. By cutting this out we not only enabled the frame of the skylight to be restored, but cleared away an obstruction to the later work of renewing the 1843 promenade saloon. The positions of the rectangular skylights were then established by laying frames of steel plate on which the wood skylights could be landed. These would also support the end of the deck planks butting against the skylights.

The positions of the aftermost three masts were in the area of the first decking stage, which meant that the special deck sockets to mate with the hingeing masts had to be made, and the first three installed in readiness. In fact these were landed on steel plates extending over three beams, to spread the load. While these final stages of preparation were in train, the ship committee was drafting a revised specification for deck laying. Partly because some of the beams were more widely spaced than those in the forecastle, and partly to achieve a deck strength more like that of the original, it was decided to incorporate an underlay of $3/4$ inch marine plywood. The plywood supplier arranged to have a $3/8$ inch thick rebate cut to a depth of two inches around the edge of each sheet, so that they could be lapped and glued to form a continuous smooth surface between the beams and the deck planks. The latter were laid on a coating of glue liberally applied to the top surface of the plywood, and then the sandwich of plank and plywood was pulled firmly down on the beams by coach screws inserted upwards through holes in the beams, most of which already existed from securing previous decks. The planks were prepared in exactly the same way as the ones selected for the forecastle, and the final touch was an application of the polysulphide rubber sealant. It seemed essential to do all this work in the dry, so the first task was to arrange for an enormous shed of scaffold tubes and corrugated iron to go up above the after end of the ship. This greatly added to the costs and we could not afford to repeat the precaution for the two later stages, but strangely in spite of all this extra care, deck leaks today are much more prevalent at the after end.

As the planking process crept steadily forward, new problems presented themselves. The first was the engine room skylight. Originally constructed of heavy timber sections, it resembles an immensely strong, low greenhouse, some 17 feet square. In due course all the components of the engine would have to enter through this skylight opening, and the sensible decision was taken to build a coaming around the opening in steel, and construct a temporary cover of scaffold tube and canvas to keep the weather out until the engine had been built. In this part of the ship the crew's galley had been built on the weather deck in 1882 and its remnants, including a brick floor laid on iron plate, had all to be dismantled and cleared.

The next items to be built and installed were the boiler room ventilators, two small ones abaft the bridge and a large one forward of the funnel. Originally these consisted of a hardwood timber coaming supporting a heavy timber grating which could be removed to enable ashes to be hoisted up for tipping overboard. With the heat of the furnaces the firemen probably welcomed an occasional shower of rain water or spray, but in the absence of any furnace heat we preferred to exclude moisture but retain the daylight. The answer was to design gratings to accept small squares of thick plate glass, watertight but not greatly changed in their appearance.

As the planking began to advance on either side of the funnel casing, we had to prepare the skylights and companionway hoods above the forward promenade saloon. The partner or deck ring for the main mast was already in position, but there remained one major alteration, the resiting of the windlass. According to the 1843 deck plan this was originally close forward of the main mast, but presumably to clear the forward cargo hold, it was moved in 1882 to a position much further forward. A steel plate bed with stiffening beneath was prepared, and then the windlass was lifted by jacks to allow small rollers to be placed under it. A temporary track of timber and plate was laid between the old and new sites and the whole assemblage, weighing several tons, was slowly dragged with a hand winch to its original home.

At last the final stage of the deck-laying began, financed by the legacy windfall noted at the end of the chapter on management, until the plank ends were butting against the break of the forecastle. After fitting a cover to the small cargo hatch dating from 1843 and the completion of the gunwale gutterways, the hull was at last watertight, and the serious restoration of the interior could begin.

Throughout the decking operation our visitors had always been given limited access to the weather deck level, and at quite an early stage they had been able to walk on a small area of the new deck. As the work neared completion visitors still had to stay behind temporary barriers until proper guardrails had been installed. From Fox Talbot's photograph of 1844 it was clear that the ship originally had a five-bar railing in iron with no timber capping, and our replacement was designed accordingly. At last all the material was to hand to complete the rails, and the great day dawned when visitors were able to enjoy the full freedom of the weather deck.

13—Masts Make a Ship

Soon after the *Great Britain* returned to Bristol, a Gloucestershire landowner offered to donate a number of trees from which new masts and spars could be made. These were to be selected from a plantation of mature Douglas firs of a size and height that suggested they would be ideal for our purpose. At once a table setting out the mast sizes was prepared, and a number of trees were earmarked to match them. Some were felled so that the trunks would be dry and seasoned by the time we were ready to step the first masts.

Traditionally a ship's masts are installed from forward to aft so in 1973, as part of the work plan for the forecastle, we prepared to install the bowsprit. This is a single timber spar 42 feet in length, jutting out beyond the prow to receive the forestay from the fore topmast. Its heel is jointed to a timber crosspiece connected between the timber bitts, and our first task was to renew these heavy posts, which had decayed beyond redemption. A single tree was then selected from the stock in the plantation and transported to Charles Hill's yard, where shipwrights were called upon to demonstrate the now rarely practised skill of shaping a spar. Gradually, under their expert hands, the rough trunk was transformed into a beautifully tapered pole which was then transported alongside the ship and hoisted onboard. Because of the absence of any lifting appliance covering the fore part of the vessel, the bowsprit then had to be man-handled up onto the forecastle with the help of rollers and simple hand-operated equipment.

As originally rigged in 1843 the *Great Britain* did not conform to any recognisable sail plan, but it must be remembered that as in the *Great Western,* sails were intended only to provide auxiliary power, when wind conditions were right, to help the continuous operation of the steam machinery. To counterbalance the large complement of engine room staff it had also been necessary to economise in the number of seamen, so the sails had to be relatively simple to handle. Against this background the ship was given six comparatively small masts, one of which had conventional square sails while the remainder carried loose-footed gaff sails, fitted with brails so that they could be furled against the masts rather like the main sail of a Thames sailing barge. Apart from the furling and reefing of the two square sails of the second or main-mast, virtually all the other sail controls could be carried out from the deck, where power assistance was provided by the hand-operated windlass at the foot of the main-mast, and by a centreline capstan between masts four and five. It has been estimated that a total of 20 seamen in two watches of 10 would have been adequate for normal steaming, but that all hands would probably have been needed during work aloft on the mainmast.

When considering the four masts abaft the funnel, the builders faced the fact that they could not be

The bowsprit supported by scaffolding as it is housed.

The topmost section of the mainmast being hoisted.

stepped on the keel in the traditional manner because of the presence of the machinery and the propeller shaft. It must also have been realised that the operation of the gaff sails would introduce sudden heavy loadings on the masts as they filled, emphasising the importance of giving the masts spring or flexibility, particularly in the fore and aft line. This led to the introduction of what we sometimes describe as 'an engineer's solution', because it hints of an element of the Brunel genius, in the form of a hinge at the foot of each mast. An iron socket mounted on the deck is connected to an iron fitting attached to the heel of the mast by means of a heavy iron pin acting as an athwartship's pivot. As a result the mast has movement fore and aft restrained only by its standing rigging, an ideal arrangement to absorb shock loadings.

Forward of the funnel the builders were able to step the two masts in the conventional manner, but since the shock forces on the gaff sail applied equally to the foremast, a hinge at deck level was also introduced. Mention has already been made of the preparation of the deck sockets for the hinged masts, but now we had to consider the problems of installing the masts themselves, the mainmast in particular.

In normal circumstances a sailing vessel is floated under a fixed or floating crane so that its masts can be lowered into position. In the case of a conventionally stepped mast like the *Great Britain's* mainmast, which passes through several decks, precision and control are essential, as the lower part of the mast descends through rings in the decks, known as partners, with only inches of clearance. But there could be no question of moving our ship, and so we had to bring the lifting equipment to it.

I now invited a number of crane hire firms to inspect our problem and quote for the work. All sent experts who arrived full of confidence, but the longer they stayed the quieter they became, until finally each in turn had to admit defeat. The position of both the fore and main masts presented a combination of three distinct difficulties: site constraints, which limited the size of crane, outreach, the distance between the crane mounting and the delivery point for the load, and the height of the lift needed for the 103 feet of the mainmast. This apparent impasse was solved firstly by the ship committee's decision that the mainmast should be made of steel tube. In contemporary paintings the mainmast is always white with black bands, in contrast to the smooth buff colour of the other five. This difference is also clear in the Fox Talbot photograph, and led us to deduce that this, the largest mast, could either have been made from the trunks of several trees banded together, or from iron plates. These would have been rolled to form separate lengths of tube connected by horizontal butt straps, the black bands portrayed in the paintings. In the absence of contemporary evidence and in the light of the advanced technology embodied in the design of the *Great Britain* it seemed reasonable to conclude that the original mainmast was indeed of iron tube, and that a replacement in steel similarly banded would be perfectly respectable. In the event the mast was split into four lengths which could be erected in succession, and connected by bolts through internal flanges

The funnel is dwarfed by the first two masts.

welded to their ends.

If we were to comply with the standard rules for masting, the foremast should have been the first to be erected. Because of its hinged foot it did not have to be lowered precisely into position, but the design of the socket meant that the hinge pin could not be inserted until the mast was at an angle of more than 60 degrees from the horizontal. In the absence of any lifting apparatus the only solution was to ignore the rigging convention, install the mainmast first, and then to use a purchase from its head to raise the head of the foremast.

The hull retained all the housings and fixtures of the three large square-rigged masts with which she ended her seagoing career in the Falkland Islands. These consisted of the large iron rings, or partners, in the decks, and a large array of iron straps, called chainplates, attached to the ship's side. The mast shrouds had been connected to these, and there was even a number of deadeyes, which are large clumps of hardwood with holes drilled through to take the rope lashings at the foot of the shrouds. For the 1843 rig all these chainplates were in the wrong position and had to be removed, but we were able to re-use most of them in our reconstruction. Some of the deadeyes could also be used for the shrouds of the mainmast, but smaller deadeyes had to be made to match the lighter rigging of the hinged masts.

As for the later mast partners, these had all to be removed in preparation for the redecking, but it had been noted that the diameter of the 1882 mizzen was the same as that of the 1843 mainmast, and a careful examination of them led to the conclusion that they were the original

partners of the mainmast, which had simply been moved aft to serve the mizzen when the ship became full-rigged in 1857. They were now moved forward to their first home as preparations began below to receive the heel of the mainmast, and it was at this point that we made the exciting discovery of a circular aperture in the surviving structure of the lowest, or orlop deck, almost exactly in the right position to accommodate our new mast. Below this an area of the tank top plating was lifted to expose part of the original duct keel, and this was carefully scaled and checked to ensure that it retained sufficient strength to support the weight of the mast.

Then came another stroke of good fortune, when the contractor who gave us the funnel offered to donate and install the mainmast. As an erector of factory chimneys, he had in his work force steeplejacks with both the skill and the equipment to put up the four steel tubes without the assistance of a crane. To me this episode proved the truth of the old naval saying that 'the impossible just takes a little longer'.

At last the four tubes arrived and preparations for their erection began. Most were concentrated on the topmost section, to which were added the heavy wooden trestle-trees and bolsters that would carry the loops of the wire rigging laid on top of them. Finally the sections were hoisted aboard by our dockside crane, and taken forward on a planked way. The team of steeplejacks then took over, and began by rigging a lattice mast and a hand winch with which they hoisted and lowered the first length of tube down into the ship through the partners. This was welded to a steel plate bolted to the duct heel, and steadied in the middle of the partners by a circle of wooden wedges. A steel panel near the bottom gave access to the inside of the tube, which was already equipped with steel rungs so that a man could climb to the top.

To add the second section to the first was comparatively simple, but after that the special skills of the steeplejacks came into their own. Their flimsy looking lattice mast was now raised by securing its heel to the second section of the mainmast with a form of saddle clamped around its circumference. Each operation was planned meticulously and executed with scarcely a word spoken. I shall never forget the way in which the fourth section, weighing more than a ton, dangled from its insubstantial hoist and was guided nonchalantly into position by men whose means of support was scarcely visible from the deck.

After the fourth section came the final touch of adding the mast cap, another component of an earlier rig. This is a heavy iron fitting like a huge pair of spectacles with one square eyepiece. The square section fits over the head of the mast, while the ring acts as a partner for an upper mast, in this case the main topmast. This weighty piece swung aloft accompanied by the foreman steeplejack, who completed the task with almost more aplomb than I can muster in recorking a bottle!

To give the mast additional strength and to make it fully watertight, the bolted joints between the tubes were continuously welded around the outside. And when the mast was painted white with black bands, as in those contemporary pictures, we stood in awe as our ship was transformed. In particular, the funnel that had previously dominated the scene paled into insignificance; the effect was almost magical, and stiffened our resolve to install the rest of the masts as quickly as our resources would allow.

By this time Charles Hill's shipyard had closed, and there was then no firm in Bristol capable of shaping masts and spars for anything bigger than a yacht. Fortunately, we had been introduced to Spencer's Rigging in Cowes, and this company was equipped to handle wire up to three inches in circumference, the size required for our main shrouds and stays. Not only was it able to take on all types of rigging work, including the production of hearts and deadeyes, but it had recently spawned a separate business to produce timber masts and spars with their iron fittings, and was well placed to meet all our requirements. As soon as our finances allowed, and spurred by a substantial donation towards the cost of a mast, we ordered a new foremast complete with topmast, gaff and all its standing rigging. At the same time an order was placed for the main topmast and the extra rigging to complete the bowsprit. With the idea of shaping the masts from solid timber, some of our donated tree trunks were transported to Cowes, but it was then decided to use their timber to build the masts from laminations with a hollow centre like some modern yacht masts. This would ensure an even quality of timber throughout, as well as reducing weight. Embodied in the design was a covered cup at the head of the mast to hold a timber preservative that would trickle slowly down the interior.

Surmounting each of the six topmasts is a round cap commonly

The main yard ready for its final movement.

The author at the wheel as No. 6 mast is prepared for installation.

called a truck. In the old days this would have been turned from a large block of wood, but we decided to make ours of metal to add durability and act as a lightning conductor. Made and donated by a friendly firm, each cap is designed to fit snugly over the head of a topmast. Its top is like a giant mushroom and houses two sheaves to take flag halyards. Once installed, the cap is connected to a copper cable running down to the ship's earthed iron hull, so there is good protection against lightning damage.

Cowes was not the most convenient spot in which to prepare the masts for a ship in Bristol. At more than 60 feet in length the foremast posed problems for road transport, and at first we thought about delivery by sea. In the end all our masts and spars travelled by special road transport from Portsmouth, where they were landed by Spencer's. The problem of crossing the Solent was solved by lowering the longer items in the sea and towing them.

So at last our foremast arrived, with its topmast, gaff and main topmast, together with all their associated rigging. Because of the awkward turns at the entrance to our yard the transporter could not be brought under our crane, so a mobile one had to be hired to off-load the mast and spars outside on Wapping Wharf. From there they were manhandled round the various bends on a handcart to arrive alongside the ship within range of our crane.

Final preparations now began with the fitting of the heel socket to the base of the mast. This is like a huge iron flower pot fitting snugly around the timber pole, but it has attached to its bottom a heavy iron bracket with a hole drilled through to take the hinge pin. The mast was then dressed with its rigging wires, and the topmast mated to it in its lowered position. The whole assembly was then hoisted aboard by our crane, and carried forward on deck by a trolley.

Since we hoped to gain maximum publicity from the dramatic event of stepping the foremast, we invited the media to witness the final stage of its being hoisted into its working position. To ensure the success of this event we planned to prepare the mast the day before, so that it would already be more than half way up, with its hinge pin inserted. At first everything went according to plan; the mast head was lifted by a purchase from the top of the mainmast until it reached an angle from which it could be further controlled by rope guys leading down to the forecastle deck, and the heel socket was successfully mated with the deck plate. Then our troubles began. To insert the hinge pin the two holes in the deck plate brackets and the hole in the heel socket bracket had to be precisely in line, but our temporary guys were not designed for such precision. Time after time the man bending low to check the alignment shouted that perfection had been achieved, but by the time the pin had started its journey through the mast had trembled. By this time dusk was falling, but we had to succeed if our demonstration to the press the next morning was to proceed according to plan. We found torches, and the struggle continued until suddenly, when the task was beginning to seem hopeless to our weary team, the shout really was one of triumph. The final setting-up of the mast the next day seemed almost an anti-climax, but its smooth completion impressed our friends from the media, who obliged with some excellent coverage on television and in the newspapers. It was as well they had not been around for the frustrations and bad language of the night before!

With the rigging of the mainmast and the hoisting of the fore and main topmasts, the fore part of the ship back to the funnel was at last to be seen in its original 1843 glory and we celebrated by hoisting the red ensign daily at the gaff on the foremast. The view of the ship from the northern side of the harbour was transformed, and it was perhaps from this moment that she finally became an accepted part of the harbour scenery. For us it was important to maintain the momentum, and plans were already being laid to step at least one mast a year to complete all six within the next four.

Although several feet longer than the foremast, No. 3 mast, or the mizzen, was installed abaft the funnel with a minimum of difficulty. Its deck plate was within the radius of our dockside crane, so the mast could be controlled precisely while the hinge pin was inserted. Then came two developments that had great bearing on the success of the masting programme. First Spencer's offered to prepare the three remaining masts under one contract, at a very fair price to be paid in a number of instalments. As this was being negotiated it was realised that mast No. 4 when in position would inhibit the working of the dockside crane, making it impossible to plumb the engine room skylight through which the parts of the replica engine would have to pass. In fact it was the shrouds that would have fouled the crane, but because of its hingeing feature the mast could not stand without them. The ship committee reluctantly concluded that the stepping of this mast would have to be deferred until all the heavy engine components had been swung aboard. It was agreed that all three masts, complete with rigging and spars, would be prepared, but that No. 4 would be stored by Spencer's until we were ready for it.

Plans now went ahead to install masts 5 and 6. Their deck sockets were outside the range of our crane, but it was possible to bring a large mobile crane into the inner end of the dock. The masts were prepared on the dockside, and then placed on board by our crane so that a mobile crane could complete the task in a working day. Everything went according to plan, and again the appearance of the ship was transformed. Even the absence of No. 4 is scarcely noticeable, and certainly does not detract from the overall impression of the vessel from afar.

When the ship operated as a floating warehouse in Port Stanley she retained her heavy lower masts as arranged in 1882 for her final rig. These are now preserved ashore, the foremast in the National Maritime Museum at Greenwich, the mizzen in Port Stanley and the mainmast alongside the ship in Bristol. To the mainmast was attached the mainyard, one of the longest ever made at 105 feet, its iron plate rolled and rivetted to form a hollow tube tapering at each end. This is also exhibited at the dock, and made me feel grateful that I was spared the greatly increased complexities of restoring this later, much heavier rig. Nevertheless, the 1843 mainyard, at some 80 feet, still

Detail of the hinge at the foot of a mast. (Photograph: The author)

had to be replaced, together with the topsail yard above it. Both these spars were constructed in timber at Cowes and delivered by road to Bristol, but the final leg of the jour-

ney into the dock again caused problems. The mainyard was the longest spar we had handled, and careful measurements had suggested that it would just clear the awkward corners between Wapping Wharf and our dockside crane. In the event, a combination of circumstances made it impossible to manoeuvre the trolley round the final bend, but the prompt arrival of a neighbour's mobile crane meant we could lift the unwieldy load, swing it around and replace it on the trolley in line with our entrance gates. After that it was simply a matter of hoisting the two yards on board, taking them forward and finally hoisting them with a hand winch.

During the masting years the fixed ensign staff was set in place at the stern, and proudly bears the red ensign every day. With so many masts it is tempting to fly a profusion of flags, but we have limited the daily display to a copy of the so-called Atlantic flag at the foremast head and one of the *Great Britain* flag at the mainmast, a combination seen in contemporary paintings.

Most people are familiar with the appearance of a three-masted square-rigged ship and many know the classic names of the masts, but even experienced mariners are baffled by the *Great Britain's* rig, and are at a loss to name the masts. It seems that this began with the shipping registrar in Bristol in 1843, who settled for 'Foremast, Mainmast, 1, 2, 3, and 4'! Even the crew seems to have had problems in identifying the masts, and adopted the simple solution of naming them after the days of the week, with Monday forward and Saturday aft. No doubt the greenhorn was asked to set sail on Sunday, to see if he would try to find a seventh mast over the stern! The conventional names for the six masts are foremast, mainmast, mizzen, jigger, driver and spanker, but for simplicity we usually refer to them in a numbered sequence from forward to aft.

After the masts were installed the next major change came with the addition of ratlines to the shrouds. Originally these were to be installed in rope, but a careful examination of Fox Talbot's photograph of 1844 suggested that they were of iron bar, perhaps more appropriate for the iron wire rigging. To reduce costs, weight and maintenance, we decided to replace them in aluminium tube anodised black, and the complete outfit was installed successfully by our own maintenance staff.

Soon after the introduction of the first three masts and their standing rigging, a theoretical investigation began into the method of handling the various sails, in particular the heavy gaffs. A detailed examination of several paintings led us to the conclusion that in the furled position the gaff sail was held close to the mast by the brails, with no part bunched below the gaff. This meant that the peak of the sail must have had an outhaul leading from a sheave or pulley near the end of the gaff, and that the head must have been supported by rings sliding along it. The evidence also pointed to the use of running rather than fixed backstays, so masts 5 and 6 reflected these important conclusions in their standing rigging, and No.'s 1 and 3 were suitably modified.

There are plans to install running rigging on one mast, together with a set of open-mesh dummy sails, so that their operation can be demonstrated. Meanwhile, the maintenance of what is already in position has added significantly to our annual budget, and there will be many days on which visitors will have the added interest of watching men working aloft.

14—'Gingerbread'

The practice of applying elaborate decorative embellishments or 'gingerbread' to a vessel goes back beyond recorded history. It has had various purposes, from superstitious to mere decoration, but by 1840 it was largely traditional. In today's functional world there is little room for such indulgences, and we would perhaps question the cost of adding useless appendages vulnerable to damage by accident or wind and wave.

For the *Great Britain,* in spite of the introduction of iron for the hull there was no break with tradition on this score, and both the bows and the stern received the close attention of carvers and gilders.

In the course of her seagoing career there were several alterations to her external decorations, and by the time she reached the Falklands in 1886 the original elaborate scheme had been reduced to the figure head, based on the national coat of arms, and some carving in the form of a hawserlaid rope framing part of the transom. Although these presumably received little care and attention after that, most of the figurehead and significant lengths of the carved ropework were still in position when the ship returned to Bristol.

At first it was thought that the figurehead could be restored, and the remaining portions were carefully detached from the hull. The unicorn was more or less complete, apart from some rot pockets, but the lion had lost its face, and half the shield between them had disappeared. Work began on the task of repair and restoration, but it soon became clear that this would be so extensive that it would be better to begin anew. To reproduce such elaborate carvings would involve a search for both the appropriate hardwood and a craftsman capable of working with it. Because of the size of such features as the lion and unicorn, it was obvious that suitable timber would present problems, while the cost of carving the embellishments would be frightening. The extra ongoing maintenance cost of preserving painted and gilded timber effectively meant accepting plastic reproductions.

Fortune then smiled on us in the shape of a local sculptor, Brian Rothnie, who offered his services and his considerable experience in the use of plastics. A room was rented from the city council at the Grove, and work began on the figurehead and the decorative features on each side of the bow, called trailboards. Brian wished to carve each feature in plasticine to form a pattern for a reproduction in glass-reinforced plastic, but the cost of plasticine in bulk meant that the larger features had to be carved out of several hundredweights of clay.

The work of reproduction from the pattern began by encasing it in plaster of paris. Once hardened this material provided the female mould, in which the finished product in glass-reinforced plastic could be laid up. This sounds relatively simple, but for the larger items such as the two beasts which are more than

Restoring the form of the prow (photograph: Cotswold Treatments Ltd), and below, the completed starboard side of the bow.

seven feet from top to toe, the task of lifting and transporting the plaster mould from the studio to the plastics factory exercised both our muscles and our ingenuity.

Meanwhile the prow or beak of the vessel was being altered back to its 1843 form, with its surfaces restored in readiness for the added decorations. After the water blasters had attacked this extremity it was a sorry sight with its stem post sticking up in front of some extremely tatty looking platework. Sufficient of the original structure remained to maintain its form, but it was obvious that this area demanded special treatment if it was to be worthy of its prominence and provide a sure foundation for the figurehead and trailboards. Fortunately the stem post itself, a magnificent example of the Victorian forgemaster's art, remained in good condition, and with the cove bars, or longitudinal butt straps, running fore and aft along the plating, it offered a strong structural skeleton on which to build. Using slender pieces of iron bar, the shipyard blacksmiths constructed a lattice framework to knit the surviving structure together and recreate the details of the curving form. To this were attached pieces of expanded metal netting to act as a foundation for a skin of plastic representing the original ship's side plating. This was prepared like a plastic dough, using chopped strands of glass fibre mixed with resin and hardener applied like plaster to the mesh and finished with a rough surface, giving the appearance of aged iron plate. Given a few coats of paint, the prow was now virtually indistinguishable from the original from alongside, but seen from above its interior was a slender wedge-shaped void. To keep out air and moisture this was filled with plastic foam topped with a small area of plastic decking finished to give the appearance of wood, and graded aft so that water would run back through a small pipe between the knightheads onto the forecastle deck.

Then came a spur in the shape of a proposed visit from Prince Philip in 1973, the highlight of which was to be the unveiling of the completed figurehead. Brian Rothnie began by preparing and mounting the trailboards, each consisting of a backboard with a shapely and decorated border, on which are mounted such motifs as a pair of meshing gear wheels and a lyre. Then followed the figurehead itself, with all its many details to be completed by the great day. As always there were inevitable setbacks caused by the weather, and when the moment came to clear the scaffolding there were still a few small pieces of gilded mouldings to be added. This was not revealed to anyone, and His Royal Highness duly admired the figurehead and expressed his pleasure at the progress achieved throughout the ship. No-one noticed that some of the mouldings at the base of the figurehead were missing; in fact they were not installed until it was regilded in 1986!

Attention was now turned to the stern, with its row of windows across the transom and dummy windows on the quarters. The window apertures were still in place but they had been boarded up, while some lengths of carved wood hawser-laid rope remained bolted to the stern. First the window openings were exposed to view by removing the boards, and the remnants of the carved rope decorations were carefully detached from the iron plating of the transom. This was then repaired and restored in preparation for its various embellishments.

The first task was to replace the stern gallery windows, the wood frames of which were shaped and fitted by the shipyard joiners and shipwrights. These had to fit the apertures in the plating, but it was discovered that none of these exactly matched, and no two frames were precisely the same size. It meant that each pane of glass was unique, and because a major manufacturer of safety glass had offered to glaze the windows free of charge, a complete set of templates had to be prepared for the factory to copy.

The decorative features at the stern presented a greater challenge than those at the bow, partly because of their complexity and partly because contemporary evidence was less precise, and even contradictory. But there was little doubt about the main decorative features on the transom, and Brian was able to proceed with their moulding and mounting on the platework under the counter. The Bristol city coat of arms is in the centre, just below the gunwale, presumably because it had been adopted as the badge of the Great Western Steam Ship Company. The badge of the Great Western Railway was the arms of the cities of London and Bristol side-by-side, so it was logical for its associated shipping company to adopt the arms of the Bristol end of the line. There have been minor changes to the design of the Bristol city arms over the years, but with the help of the city archivist and the curator of the Swindon Railway Museum, we were able to use the 1843 arms for our reproduction.

Other features produced and in-stalled at the same time were palm fronds to port and starboard above the windows, and bunches of oak leaves between them. The production of the latter involved the need for repetitive items for the first time, and we were fortunate to be able to use a company specialising in this art. All that then remained to be added were the borders of carved rope, the upper lengths representing ordinary three-strand and the bottom border hawser-laid. We had the remains of the original carved wood of the latter to copy, but could not at first decide the easiest and cheapest method of reproducing the features. Because of their layout and of the curving surface of the transom it was impossible to use repeats of a standard length. At about this time, partly through the hard work of a group of local supporters calling themselves the Bristol Committee of Friends of the s.s. *Great Britain*, relations between the project and the city council showed distinct signs of improvement, and it was agreed to mark this by inviting the Lord Mayor to make a formal visit. What could be more appropriate for him to unveil than the stern decorations surmounted by the city coat of arms? The work was finished quickly without the rope borders, so that the scaffolding could be removed in time for the ceremony, and so it was that like his royal predecessor at the bow, the Lord Mayor unveiled the decorated stern almost certainly unaware that the work had yet to be completed. The equipment for the unveiling consisted of a large black plastic curtain hanging from the gunwale, which had to fall into the dock bottom when the Lord Mayor pulled a rope. This presented me with a few headaches, not least the

Final touches around the unicorn, and below, the transom ready for restoration.

protruding horns of the two unicorns supporting the city arms, which threatened to hook themselves under the sheet. There was neither the time nor the labour to come up with a more sophisticated release arrangement, so on the day I lay prone on the deck at the stern and as the Lord Mayor pulled the rope, lifted the sheet clear of obstructions to fall cleanly. This explains why I do not appear in the photographs taken on this occasion!

Partly as a result of this interruption, and partly because other items of restoration were given higher priority, progress at the stern came to a halt, and I temporarily lost contact with the sculptor Brian Rothnie. Then, nearly two years later, he called without warning to announce that he had become involved in community service work, and suggested that we might be able to include the decorations in a job creation scheme. To win approval from the Manpower Services Commission, which provided all funding, we had to prepare a clearly defined programme that would offer work experience of a precise nature. We decided to go for the production of items using our proven techniques, and avoid experiments on the carved ropes and work on scaffolding. We proposed that two young unemployed artists should be employed under Brian to complete the task of modelling the two flying swans that were a prominent feature of the original quarter galleries. They appear to be flying out of the ship so that their wings are spread fully with a span of about nine feet; since each is a mirror image of the other, separate models had to be carved out of plasticine for each side. Contemporary paintings and Fox Talbot's photograph were used to interpret the various details of the birds, and the whole experience was an excellent practical challenge to which the two young artists responded with enthusiasm. After many months of painstaking work the two models were ready to be encased in plaster of Paris to make the moulds, and shortly afterwards two fine glass-reinforced plastic swans were ready to be installed on the ship.

Sadly, our budget at that time could not cover expenditure on decorative features, so it was decided to install the swans alone, approximately correctly positioned, as a temporary move to show off this further evidence of progress.

At last, in 1980, we were able to fund the completion of the stern decorations, beginning with much discussion of the details of the quarter galleries, based on various contemporary sources of evidence. Once again we were fortunate to have the services of Brian Rothnie, who began by preparing design proposals for consideration by the ship committee. Varied evidence meant that there was inevitably some difference of opinion, but eventually a British compromise emerged, offering a satisfactory appearance, ease of construction and minimal maintenance.

Work began on the transom to complete the rope borders, and at my suggestion Brian used an actual length of three-stranded rope to develop his mould. A mould for a length of hawser-laid rope was made from the surviving piece of original carved wood, and then the sculptor developed his own technique for preparing and shaping short lengths to be applied to the hull and joined to create the continuous borders of the decorations.

Attention then turned to the quarter galleries, where again some border decorations were of the rope design. The layout of the entire scheme was marked on the plate-work, when it was found necessary to adjust the position of the two swans. The design of the dummy windows on the quarters had been interpreted from both the Fox Talbot photograph and contemporary paintings. There was strong evidence to suggest that there were curved glass panes in these windows, but in the interests of economy of production and maintenance, glass was omitted from our design; the illusion of windows was limited to our use of raised frames with the window apertures simply painted in blue.

Another major feature on the quarters is the pair of cornucopiae which soften the corners between the quarters and the transom. Again these had to be produced individually to fit snugly against the somewhat irregular shape of the hull at this point. We used a new technique involving a block of plastic material in the rough shape of a cornucopia being mounted in its final position before the sculptor carved in the final details. It was then coated with resin to seal it and give it a durable surface that could be gilded and painted.

Another item researched at length was the original name painted on the hull. Evidence was limited, but it all pointed to the use of 'The Great Britain', presumably to differentiate it from the country. This was carved on a suitable length of hardwood, and the letters were finished in gold leaf before the board was put up on the transom. Beneath it was placed a second carved board naming the port of registration as Bristol, in accordance with the legal requirements in force in 1843.

It only remained to add various small decorative carvings of oak leaves and mouldings and to complete the gilding and painting, and the stern decorations were at last in place. But though this complex and specialised task was now behind us, the decoration of the interior seemed likely to present even greater challenges in the future.

15—Starting the Engine

Considering the extremities of corrosion and decay throughout the hull on its return, and the slender financial resources available, it is understandable that the restoration of the engine then seemed an impossible dream. But the basic decision made had been to restore the vessel as far as practicable to its 1843 state, when it was a screw-driven steamship, and the heart of that ship was undoubtedly the engine. Many early visitors inquired about it, and a few enthusiasts were already researching its design.

When the ship ran aground in Dundrum Bay in 1846 the engine sustained only minor damage. But its many months on the beach saw the engine room flooded, and the machinery must have been in a sorry state on return to Liverpool after the salvage. When the ship was laid up awaiting a purchaser the engine no doubt suffered from further neglect, and it was probably beyond economical repair by the time of her sale in January 1851. But other influences led to the scrapping of her original machinery. There would always be spare parts problems in a unique engine built by a now defunct company and besides, there had been dramatic improvements in the design of marine steam plant over the past ten years. Crucially, the ship's role was to be changed from that of a steamship with auxiliary sails to a sailing ship with an auxiliary steam engine, so the new owners were more than happy to change to one of the standard engines built by Penn,

with two oscillating cylinders, a geared drive onto the shaft and the capacity to develop a mere 500 horsepower. To reduce the drag created by a stationary propeller when sailing, the shaft was fitted with a clutch to let the screw revolve freely, but the idea was not an outstanding success, and in 1857 it was scrapped in favour of a widely used lifting propeller system.

This involved a major modification at the stern, with a large vertical frame like two goal posts set in line behind the original stern post and a watertight trunk or shaft of iron plate extending from the underside of the stern to the topmost deck. A smaller iron frame was designed to fit in the vertical frame, with sliding shoes to let it move up and down in the manner of a sash window. A two-bladed Griffiths propeller was mounted on bearings housed in the sliding frame, and with the frame fully lowered it could be connected to the propeller shaft by a sliding clutch operated from inboard. When sails alone were used the propeller was declutched and hoisted clear of the water into the trunk.

All these technical features and developments represent important milestones in the history of the ship and of marine engineering generally, and it is obviously a part of the project's function to record all available details and inform the public. But the decision to opt for the 1843 design meant that any plans to restore the machinery must be based on the original four-cylinder engine developed by Brunel, while our aim to recreate the after promenade saloon meant we had to cut out and remove all traces of the lifting propeller trunk at the upper 'tween deck level; a small portion remains below that deck. The massive bedplate of the Penn engine remains in the ship, but it will be virtually buried beneath a restored 1843 engine, and will partly support it.

In the early years I received occasional visits from representatives of engineering firms interested in the ship's machinery, and sometimes they offered help, but in the absence of adequate drawings it was difficult to get anything started. Then, in 1976, an initiative was led by Lord Strathcona, a member of our project council, and Mr. Gordon Victory, the then president of the Institute of Marine Engineers, to form a group of enthusiasts to sponsor the construction of a full-scale replica of the original machinery. At first this was intended to be a separately funded project to provide job opportunities for young people in 1977, the Queen's Silver Jubilee year, and its early title was the s.s. Great Britain Jubilee Engine Replica Project.

Wide-ranging publicity was given to it, but in spite of numerous offers of practical help from industry, cash donations were few; almost from the beginning the engine project received modest financial support from the s.s. Great Britain Project itself.

The engine project began with high hopes of completing the construction in about two years, which might have been possible if a complete set of contemporary drawings had existed and it had proved practicable to rebuild to exact original specifications. Unfortunately, although a folio of contemporary engravings published by Weale remained available in a few reference libraries, these did not cover every part of the engine, and were not adequate for detailed work. Weight was another factor. The original engine weighed some 350 tons, but it was obviously desirable to make the replica as light as possible, and a target weight of less than 100 tons was set. At length it was decided that although the replica would not be capable of steaming, it should portray accurately the original in every visible detail, and be capable of rotation by an independent power source; it could be constructed of any suitable modern materials.

Today a ship's engine is built as a complete unit and supplied to the shipyard to be hoisted on board and landed on a prepared bedplate, but the *Great Britain's* engine was built into the ship so that, for example, its main crankshaft was supported in bearings at the upper 'tween deck level, while its four cylinders were mounted on special bedplates in the turn of the bilge to port and starboard. The framework, which carried the main moving parts of the engine, consisted of a number of heavy timber beams spanning the machinery space, with integral angled legs from the weather deck to the bilge, like a gigantic letter A. In accordance with contemporary practice, the fore and aft sides of the timbers were faced with iron plate, bolted firmly in place. Apart from their primary function, the engine frames provided structural strength to the ship, and this meant that the frames of our replica had to perform this task for real. The constraints of weight, and availability of suitable wood meant that our frames were designed as hollow steel fabrications which could be disguised with timber cladding on the horizontal surfaces and steel plates on the vertical to give a fair representation of the original.

One of the engine project's first needs was to obtain the services of a design engineer, and again fortune smiled on us in the person of a retired Royal Naval engineer, James Richard, whose hobby seemed to be the study of early steam machinery. It was quickly apparent that we had found a person with the knowledge and ability to help us, and at first he shared the euphoria that still motivated the engine committee. But it was obvious to me that financial constraints alone would delay the essential alterations to the ship itself for several years, a view which James indirectly supported by explaining to the committee the magnitude of the total design effort in prospect. Apart from the need to study the many gaps in the 1843 design information and to draw up basic designs based on the best contemporary knowledge available, virtually every part of the machinery had to be redesigned for modern manufacture, starting with the main frames.

The appeal had produced few offers of help with design and drawing work, most of which failed to perform, and the committee realised that lack of drawings seemed likely to be their downfall. For example, many firms who had offered practical help were likely to lose interest if they had to wait many months for drawings of components they had agreed to make as a donation. Against this background, James Richard applied himself with vigour to the design task, and with a minimum of help produced not only a set of basic drawings but a simply constructed scale model which would assist with both the progressive design of components and an understanding of the whole machine by those offering to manufacture parts. As a result of his efforts many firms were able to begin work, at which point I had to contemplate the problem of storing engine components in our dockside warehouse.

At first the motivation of the engine project depended on the efforts of the original group of enthusiasts, who met regularly at the Institute of Marine Engineers in London, under the chairmanship of Lord Strathcona. The then chairman of the Great Britain Project, Richard Goold-Adams, and myself were members of this committee, and it was partly due to our influence that the need was seen to relate the engine development more closely with that of the ship. Apart from the installation of the engine frames, which would involve some alterations to the ship's structure, the whole layout of the central area of the vessel had to be considered, both in relation to the original and to accommodate an engine intended largely to be a public exhibit. These were obviously matters to be resolved by the ship committee. So the logical step was taken to form an engine subcommittee to control the design, construction and installation of the engine components. With a membership consisting mostly of qualified engineers of various disciplines, including James Richard, this committee has held regular meetings in Bristol since October 1978, and has ensured continuity of effort on this major development. Although the separate engine project was not formally ended, from then on the Great Britain Project took financial responsibility for the engine.

The project engineer, Alan Skidmore, with one of four pairs of crosshead guides, give some idea of the size of the engine components. (Photograph: The author)

Now came yet another stroke of good fortune when one of the senior draftsmen of Charles Hill and Sons, made redundant by the closure of the firm, agreed to produce drawings to detail the structural alterations to the midship area. In conjunction with James Richard I prepared outline proposals for the approval of the ship committee, and these rapidly became drawings for the guidance of our contractor. The idea was to replace the original iron plate deck of the upper 'tween level in steel, and to rebuild the coal bunkers to port and starboard of the machinery space. More or less at the same time the design of the four engine frames was being finalised, and money was allocated to enable the central pair of frames, which support the crankshaft, to be ordered. We hoped that the ship would be ready to receive them when they were delivered a year later, but this proved impossible, and in due course I had to find a temporary home in a disused tobacco warehouse for a set of meccano weighing some 28 tons! A major start had been made, however, and from then on progress was to be simply a question of keeping design and drawing work ahead of the installation schedule.

16—In the Engine Room

The year 1876 was the last in which the now elderly hull felt the thump of engines and the beat of a propeller. When she was laid up at Birkenhead it was not only the end of an era, but was doubtless regarded by many as the end of the s.s. *Great Britain*. In fact her destiny lay elsewhere, following her conversion in 1882 from a passenger liner into a bulk cargo ship propelled by sails alone. Her hull now contained three large holds, the centre one occupying the entire space originally given up to the machinery, and the 1852 Penn engine that had given 24 years of service on voyages throughout the world was unceremoniously scrapped, leaving only its bedplate by way of epitaph. A similar fate befell the boilers, together with the coal bunkers and all the auxiliary machinery. The huge void left was criss-crossed by a forest of new beams and pillars for strength.

Once the decision to install a full-scale replica of the engine of 1843 had been taken, our first task was to decide the best method of modifying the 1882 beams and pillars to recreate the engine space without hazarding the ship's structural stability, and preferably without interrupting the flow of visitors. At that time, public access to spaces below the weather deck was limited, and our plans had to be changed to include facilities to view the engine. Research of contemporary drawings and records indicated that the upper 'tween deck above the boiler room was originally made of iron plate, so we began by planning to replace this deck level, including the gallery decks to port and starboard of the engine, in steel. Below the gallery decks were coal bunkers with inclined longitudinal inner surfaces lying close above the engine cylinders to port and starboard.

As for the engine room itself, it was decided that to create the illusion of reality, all the boundaries of the space should be reconstructed. Apart from the after bulkhead which had already been restored, this decision meant that the after end of the boiler and the port and starboard coal bunkers would all have to be rebuilt. At the same time it was decided that the rest of the inside spaces in the central part of the vessel would be developed largely with visitors in mind, to provide the maximum space to view the engine from every possible angle. Apart from the engine room and possibly selected exhibits such as a dummy cooking range, no attempt would be made to recreate the nineteenth-century layout in this part of the vessel.

The next step was to prepare drawings setting out the alterations that had to be completed before the installation of the engine could be contemplated. At first these were to include the replacement of the upper 'tween deck above the boiler space, and the gallery decks already mentioned. The latter were originally separated from the engine room by longitudinal bulkheads, but in our reconstruction these were to be reduced to bulwarks capped with wood, providing balconies running fore and aft from which the machinery could be viewed. As the drawings were being prepared it was suggested that by laying steel decks in the coal bunkers at the lower 'tween level and cutting windows in the bunker faces we could create an additional viewing level for visitors. The drawings were modified accordingly, together with the addition of stairways to port and starboard leading to the deck above.

At last work began on laying the plating at the upper 'tween level, including the gallery or side decks abreast the engine room. An immediate benefit for visitors was the creation of a large concourse below decks in the fore part of the ship, from which stairways led to the weather deck. Then came another dramatic intervention, when the Gas Board offered to build the dummy boiler front using workers under training. At first we had given this feature lower priority than the engine itself, and our plans had been limited to the construction of a steel bulkhead on which the dummy face of the boiler would later be mounted. Forward of this bulkhead the space originally filled by the boiler would be left void, leaving visitors to imagine the enormous size of the 'kettle' required to produce the steam!

An immediate change in priorities allowed a prompt start to be made on the support structure for the boiler face and the preparation of drawings of the face itself, including all the pipework and controls. Fortunately the Weale engravings included reasonably detailed drawings of the boiler, so little research was needed before our draftsman could begin. Some of the features of the boiler front, such as water gauge glasses, had to be purpose made, but it proved possible to use modern gas piping to represent most of the pipework of the feedwater and brine systems, while the twelve furnace doors were adapted from retort doors taken from redundant coal gas plant. In the early days of steam propulsion at sea it was impossible to produce fresh water for the boilers, so they had to accept sea water. Of course the salt separated out to form dense brine which inhibited the production of steam, and this had to be constantly removed by a system of pipes leading out to the sea. To save some of the heat from the boiling brine, it was passed through a heat exchanger in which it warmed the cold feed water on its way to the feed tank above the boiler. Fortunately, the donation of a reproduction heat exchanger coincided neatly with the construction of the boiler front, and the proper pipe connections could be made.

During work on the boiler, the ship committee gave careful thought to the preparation of the ship's structure to accommodate the loads that would be imposed by the four engine frames and the various components. As designed, the engine framework was built to carry the various loads imposed by the heavy rotating masses both when the vessel was in calm water and when she was rolling and pitching. In these circumstances the submerged surface of the hull is supported by sea pressure offering a relatively even distribution of loads, but in the unnatural situation of a dry dock conditions are totally different. The whole weight of the *Great Britain* is borne on its main and docking keels, plus a few extra dock blocks placed at selected points below the hull. In the absence of sea pressure

The supports for the crankshaft between which the chain wheel will revolve. (Photograph: The author)

the ship's side plating and deck edge loads virtually hang on the internal frames, and the pillars between decks remain an essential part of the structural integrity.

Against this background it was decided that the framework of the replica engine must be designed so that most of its weight would be transferred vertically through the keels to the dock bottom, and that it would help to support the overhang of the ship's sides, rather than the reverse. Noting that the inner legs of the A frames landed on the tank top plating directly above the docking keels, it was agreed that these should sustain the entire vertical load. To prepare the ship to accept this, two longitudinal girders of reinforced concrete were installed over the length of engine, in contact with the hull plating above the docking keels.

In accordance with contemporary practice, the cylinders and steam valves of the original engine were lagged to reduce heat losses and encased in wood which extended almost the full length of the bedplate on which the cylinders and their valve chests were mounted. In terms of our model, this arrangement offered the advantages that none of the hidden components would need to be designed or constructed, and that the casing could be mounted on the 1882 tank top plating without detracting from its appearance. Then we decided that interest in the engine as an exhibit would be greatly increased if one pair of cylinders was displayed without its casing, which meant that an area of the tank top would have to be removed to enable a dummy bedplate to be fitted. The tank top is a plated surface forming the floor of the hold, and since it is connected both to iron girders below and to the ship's side plating, it contributes to the overall strength of the hull. To compensate for the removal of a substantial section on the starboard side, it was agreed to install a number of stiffening brackets of steel to selected frames in the turn of the bilge. These were set at an angle that allowed them to act also as supports for the cylinder bedplate.

The main engine beams for the model, incorporated in the frames at both upper and lower 'tween deck levels, were designed to connect to beams extending to the ship's sides. Since these would become the sole ship's beams at this point, it was important that they connected to sound frames, and many of these had to be renewed. Many visitors comment on the beautiful curving form of the hull which must, of course, be followed by the internal framing. We then discovered that after the closure of Charles Hill there was no firm in Bristol capable of bending steel angles to our requirements, so we had to use a works in Birmingham.

All these repairs and alterations in the engine room area occupied our contractor's work force for many months, and ate up a great deal of money without giving our visitors any visual indication of progress. The first pair of engine frames had long since arrived, adding to the impatience of the engine subcommittee, but we had reached only the end of the beginning, and the preparations continued with the rebuilding of the longitudinal bulkheads forming the inner faces of the coal bunkers. Embodied in these was the plate deck at the lower 'tween level on which visitors would view the engine from the bunkers.

At long last the structural preliminaries were complete, and the installation of the first engine frame could be contemplated. These had been designed and built as a bolted assembly, and delivered to Bristol as large kits of parts which had to be placed on board in correct order for final assembly. A start was made with the beams of the central pair of frames, and since these support the main bearing of the crankshaft, they had to be located with absolute precision. After many months of careful work the greater part of all four frames had been installed and connected both to the ship's sides and to the weather deck, allowing us to consider the removal of the beams and pillars of 1882.

To the casual observer the empty engine room probably seemed to offer ample space, but a drawing reveals that the original machinery fitted with only inches to spare. With components so tightly packed, the order of assembly had to be defined carefully in an erection schedule, and this now guides the work programme and helps to ensure that components are given priority in design and construction to meet installation targets.

At the time of writing the bedplate for the starboard cylinders is about to be laid down, and then it will be possible to place in position the two cylinders, seven feet four inches in diameter, with their associated valve chests. Our visitors should be able to see this important development from the new viewing galleries, and follow each step of the realistic reproduction of a historic piece of Victorian machinery.

79

17—The Propeller and Rudder

Brunel's proposal to introduce a screw propeller involved several dramatic alterations to plans for the engine, and for the ship's stern and structure, generally. As a paddle steamer a simple rudder was planned behind a plain stern post, but now this post had to be modified to include a tube for a shaft and the rudder had to be moved aft, clear of the propeller. The ship's keel line was extended by a plate shoe or skeg to support a post around which turned a balanced rudder of modern appearance which gave the ship exceptionally light steering control. The upper part of the aperture was modified to create a square opening, in which the six-bladed propeller would revolve. In the early days of screw propulsion the stern bearing was a major problem, with its brass bushes wearing rapidly, but in the *Great Britain* Brunel installed the stern bearing abaft the stern post, so that it was water lubricated and cooled, and the bushes could be changed fairly easily in dry dock.

After that, of course, come the various alterations to the propulsion system following the ship's change of role from Atlantic liner to auxiliary steam clipper to Australia. These culminated in the installation of a lifting propeller system in 1857 until finally, when the ship was converted to carry cargo alone and reverted to sail power, the propeller was removed and the aperture plated over in 1882. This was the form of the stern that remained, together with a simple, unbalanced rudder, when the ship docked in Bristol in 1970.

With so much first aid work demanding our attention and resources, the restoration of even such a significant feature as the propeller was not high on our list of priorities, but then we received an offer from a leading manufacturer to make a replica as a donation. We immediately investigated the existing state of the stern frame to assess the full extent of the task of restoring this area to its 1843 layout. We discovered, for example, that the 1857 frame for the lifting propeller was substantially intact, but fairing plates forward of it hid the position of the 1843 stern post, leaving us unsure of its existence or condition.

Instructions were first given to the shipyard to remove the blanking plates from the 1857 aperture, and this revealed the frame of the lifting propeller system in perfect condition. This frame, built from heavy forgings of varying cross sections up to two feet by eleven inches, was connected to the ship at the keel and by two posts built up into the counter of the stern. The expense of removing this and restoring the stern aperture was obviously going to be a major item on our budget, and we decided to defer it; but the arrival of the replica of the original six-bladed propeller was imminent, and it seemed ungrateful to the donor to park it at the dockside. We then found it possible to hoist it temporarily into the 1857 aperture, supported on a length of steel tube inserted through its hub. This method of exhibiting the propeller

Top: The reproduction 1845 propeller supported in the 1857 frame with the original stern post exposed.

Bottom: The propeller moved aside and the 1857 frame cut free and placed by the dock wall.

Reconstruction of the shape of the propeller aperture by adding a dummy extension.

resulted in the disadvantage that, in spite of an explanatory notice, a succession of 'experts' called at the office to advise me that the propeller could not revolve because it was too big for the aperture! I like to think they were handled with tact, and left feeling that they had made an important contribution.

At last, in 1976, I began to study the task of converting the propeller aperture back to its 1843 form, stimulated by the urgent need for the tailshaft, which had to be lowered into the after hold before the weather deck was laid. As originally designed the propeller shafting was made up of three sections: at the forward end a solid length of drive-shaft extending from the engine through the after engine room bulkhead; at the after end another solid length forming the tailshaft; and in between, a connecting torque tube of rolled iron plate some 61 feet in length, a remarkable feat of engineering for the period.

We decided that even if we succeeded in installing a rotatable engine, a rotating propeller would introduce unacceptable hazards to people visiting the dock bottom, so the design of the tailshaft was simplified. The aftermost section was machined exactly as the original from a solid bar and finished with a tapered end and nut to mate with the propeller, and the remaining length was made from standard steel tube welded to the solid portion. Once on board, the tapered end was to be presented to the propeller from inboard through the stern tube, while the forward end was finally to be held by steel bands bolted firmly to heavy timbers which originally supported the forward bearing of the tailshaft.

The 1857 alterations had brought extensive structural changes, and there was some anxiety that their complete reversal might lead to serious weakening of the hull and an undesirable amount of replacement of original ironwork. We settled for a compromise enabling us to recreate the external appearance while accepting the impossibility of restoring all the interior to its original layout. The plated vertical trunk for the lifting propeller dominated the after end of the upper 'tween deck level and passed down to mate with the hull plating. Below the upper 'tween level the forward face of the trunk was continued to port and starboard to form an athwartship bulkhead, a feature we were anxious to preserve. Our final decision was to modify the structure to enable the original extent of the promenade saloon to be restored, but not to disturb any structure below. This involved some curtailment at the after end of the dining saloon, including the after stairways.

Work began with the careful removal of the propeller trunk between the upper 'tween level and the weather deck, including the two posts of the lifting frame. Pillars were positioned between the decks, and new lengths of beam spanned the open top of the trunk. When it was done we saw for the first time the full beauty of the stern gallery as originally conceived.

Externally there was no alternative to the complete removal of the 1857 frame, and at first there were fears that, with the ship in dock, it might be supporting the overhang of the stern. Substantial timber shores were placed in position below the counter before any work was begun. As explained earlier, fairing plates were riveted in position between the

The balanced rudder completes the restoration at the stern. (Photograph: The author)

old stern and the 1857 frame, hiding the original stern post. Removing these plates without damaging the hull plating behind them was a slow and tedious task, but we were rewarded by the sight of Brunel's 1843 stern post, apparently in perfect condition, with two external rounded flanges still in position to hold the external bearing.

Now began the detailed planning of the structural work to be carried out, including the removal of the 1857 frame and the construction and installation of a skeg and rudder post which formed part of the alteration of the propulsion from paddles to a screw. The plating over the bottom of the propeller trunk in 1882 created a hull line sloping upwards towards the stern, but a careful check revealed that at the forward end of the aperture the clearance for the propeller remained as built in 1843. In planning the removal of the 1857 frame we decided to cut the forward leg flush with the hull plating and the after leg at the same horizontal level; they could then be used later to align and support the reconstruction of the square aperture of 1843.

The solepiece of the 1857 frame was finished at its forward end to a deep U shape, to fit snugly around the base of the 1843 stern post and the ship's hull plating. It was secured by closely spaced long rivets passing from side to side, and its release from the hull presented a formidable challenge. Fortunately, it was found possible to connect the restoration soleplate without disturbing this part of the 1857 solepiece, and at long last, in 1981, work was able to begin.

The reproduction propeller weighs about four tons, and had first to be moved out of its temporary home in the 1857 frame. We wished to avoid slinging heavy weights from the overhanging counter and I devised a scheme to remove the propeller horizontally, supported by a framework of scaffolding tubes. Two frameworks were built from the stern frame to the dock wall, connected at the base and each topped by a line of timber planks. Once these were in place the tube supporting the propeller was freed from its securing straps, and the propeller was easily moved sideways by rotating it by hand so that the support tube travelled along the planks, while the blades passed between the frameworks. Once against the dock wall the propeller was secured, and the inner ends of the support frames were cleared from the stern frame structure.

We were then ready to remove the 1857 frame, which had to be preserved with its rudder as a historic exhibit in its own right. The task resolved itself into two phases, the separation of the frame by making three cuts through the heavy forgings of the two legs and solepiece, and the removal of the seven-ton structure to the side of the dock opposite the propeller, where it could remain permanently on display. Again we were fortunate when friendly contractors offered specialists in oxy-acetylene burning and in moving objects under precise control.

The condition of the forgings was excellent and the cuts were ex-ecuted with precision accompanied by a steady stream of molten iron which solidified in a misshapen heap on the dock floor. As the frame was released from the ship it was stabilised by wires and purchases that held it upright and then, with the aid of hydraulic jacks, its weight was transferred to two shoes like flat roller skates. Travelling slowly along two temporary steel tracks, the frame at last came to rest alongside the dock wall, where it was secured.

Now our solepiece or skeg, forming the base of the propeller aperture, was attached to the keel in the way it had been done under Brunel's direction in 1840, when the propulsion system was altered half way through building. A replacement for the eight inch diameter angled rudder post was forged in carbon manganese steel as a donation from a friendly firm and cranked at its upper end to conform to the original. We had established by measurement that the stump of the after leg of the 1857 frame, protruding below the counter, was in exactly the right position to receive the upper end of the rudder post. The lower end of this was housed in a socket or cup riveted to the after end of the soleplate.

In considering the problem of re-creating the original square form of the propeller aperture, we decided to try to avoid cutting away part of the existing hull plating, which might tend to weaken the structure of the counter. Instead, a steel framework was developed using the stump of the after leg of the 1857 frame as a strongpoint, and to this was attached a falsepiece, or dummy section of hull plating. This was so skilfully formed and attached that it gives the visitor a totally realistic and convincing impression.

Although it is planned to rotate the engine, the propeller will not be connected to it and will remain static. This meant that the external bearing, mounted behind the stern post, could be a dummy, and the weight of the propeller on its shaft could be taken directly by the stern post, via timber packing around the shaft.

At last all was ready for the propeller, and the full length of the scaffolding framework was rebuilt with its two timber trackways. The tailshaft was presented from inboard and wedged in its operating position, and then the propeller was carefully aligned with the shaft and moved forward, complete with its tube axle, so that the screwed end of the shaft entered the tube. Using hydraulic jacks, the propeller was inched forward, sliding from its support tube on to the tapered end of the shaft until it was fully home. The operation was completed by the fixing of the propeller nut, followed by its cover plate.

All that now remained to be restored was the balanced rudder, originally made of heavy iron forgings and iron plate. We plumped for a replica made of glass-reinforced plastic and designed in the form of two half shells which could be offered up to port and starboard of the rudder post and then bonded together. To simplify construction the bearings would be dummies, and the rudder would be set permanently in the fore and aft position. Drawings were prepared and a boatbuilder who specialised in craft with plastic hulls undertook the work. Finally, in 1987, the rudder was in place, and after eleven years of painstaking work, the stern of the ship once again presented the appearance that must have amazed so many observers before the ship was launched in 1843. No doubt even Brunel himself once stood on the dock floor to contemplate his handiwork, confident that his theoretical calculations would be borne out by practical trials.

18—A Touch of Luxury

As the work upon the exterior of the ship neared its end, attention was diverted to the problems of restoring the interior. One of our first aims was to recreate enough passenger accommodation to let the visitor visualise what life might have been like on board a liner in the mid-nineteenth century, and we had generally agreed that this could be achieved by restoring the accommodation spaces, including a few cabins, at the after end.

Against a background of modern cruise liners and holiday hotels, it is difficult to appreciate that the facilities offered to passengers on board the *Great Western* and *Great Britain* were luxurious by contemporary standards. Compared with many sailing packets which offered private facilities to a minority, the blocks of cabins seemed limitless; indeed, these were the very beginnings of the concept of a liner as a floating hotel, an image borne out by the high standard of catering and the provision of water closets, a luxury possessed by few houses and hotels at that date!

As originally constructed, the ship had two complete accommodation units separated by the machinery compartment amidships. Each unit was arranged on two decks, the upper consisting of a central leisure or promenade area with blocks of cabins on either side, and the lower with three long tables forming a central dining area, again with cabins on the outboard sides. At the promenade level the cabin blocks were separated from the public area by partitions called screen bulkheads. Doors in these led to short passageways running out to the ship's side, from which opened two inboard and two outboard cabins. A similar layout was repeated at the level below, but because of the reducing width of the ship both forward and aft, some cabins opened directly from the saloon. Another feature was the provision of two small state rooms for ladies, from each of which opened two private two-berth cabins, a perfect arrangement for those travelling unaccompanied by a male escort. The state rooms also had an attendant stewardess and access to private water closets, so it was possible for ladies to travel the width of the Atlantic without being embarrassed by the company of gentlemen!

Altogether there were 252 berths for passengers in cabins, and provision for a number of passengers to sleep on settees in the public rooms. It is generally accepted that the after accommodation unit was for first class and the forward for second class passengers, although the charges, ranging from 20 to 35 guineas, seem to have been related directly to the standard of berth, as in a modern liner. The settees were probably occupied by the valets and ladies' maids of the predominantly wealthy travellers of the time.

By today's standards the cabins were minute, mostly little more than six feet square for two persons, but at the time the provision of such privacy and especially the comfort of proper bed spaces with sheets and pillows, would have been regarded as the height of luxury. Each cabin had a small washbowl which emptied into a hidden bucket below. Stewards brought hot and cold water for washing each morning, a system which prevailed in some ocean liners well into the twentieth century. The deck plans make no mention of bathrooms, but it is assumed that a certain number of hip baths were carried, and could be provided in a cabin on request.

The passenger's days, as in modern liners, were punctuated by meals: breakfast, a light luncheon and a main dinner in the early evening. No exact details of the cooking facilities have survived, but a visitor to the ship described them as extensive, like those of a first class hotel. Evidence suggests that they were grouped around the funnel uptake on the upper 'tween deck level. The smoke from the galley stoves would then have poured into the main funnel, while steam for culinary purposes would have been readily available from the boiler room below. From the galley, food was conveyed by stewards forward and aft, and down one deck to the two dining saloons where there were pantries with serving hatches.

Before the invention of improved oil lamps, artificial lighting below decks was provided largely by spermaceti candles and lamps burning colza oil. The level of illumination would not be tolerated today, but it was probably as good as most of the passengers were used to at home. With so many naked flames the risk of fire was ever-present, and there were stringent rules for extinguishing all lights except for night lights at a fixed hour every evening. It was obviously important to provide for the maximum natural light during the day, and this was achieved by the generous provision of skylights above the promenade saloons, and portholes in almost every outboard cabin. The weather deck was breached by no fewer than 18 openings for rectangular skylights, ten above the after and eight above the forward promenade saloons. In addition, the after saloon had a magnificent circular skylight to provide extra light to the stern gallery.

To take light to the dining saloons each rectangular skylight was duplicated by a similar opening in the promenade saloon deck. Evidence suggests that these had wooden frames with top openings protected by thin bars, probably of brass. Not only did they provide light, but they helped with the ventilation of the dining saloon. Finally, the after dining saloon was also served by a circular skylight in the promenade deck, exactly below the one in the weather deck.

Just as all the weather deck skylights had to be installed before laying the deck planking, now the skylights above the after dining saloon had to be set in place before the planking of the promenade saloon could begin. We were lucky to have an offer from the Bristol Skill Centre to make the ten rectangular skylight frames as a training task, meaning we had to pay only for the materials.

Our stock of second-hand pitch-pine planking was still sufficient to complete the entire after promenade saloon, but after cleaning and planing the planks their maximum uniform thickness was only $2^1/4$ inches, compared with the four-inch planks of the original deck. As a result the beams were found to be too far apart, and a number of additional

Top: The beams and pillars of the promenade saloon altered in readiness for decklaying.

Bottom: Decklaying proceeds at the promenade level with dining room skylights already in place.

The forward end of the promenade saloon showing the main entrances and cabin bulkheads on each side. (Photograph: The author)

intermediate ones had to be added. While fitting these, areas of weakness were discovered at the ship's side, hidden in the patent box stringers or longitudinal stiffeners added in the 1860's to strengthen the hull. As these did not form part of the 1843 construction they were removed from the after part of the ship.

When the cabins were dismantled in 1882 a large number of beams were strengthened by new ones in the recently invented T bulb section, and the pillars throughout both the promenade and dining saloon spaces were rearranged. The revised layout of pillars was incompatible with the interior plan of 1843, and we were faced with the task of moving virtually every single one back to its original position. Since these were all load-bearing, this job had to be carried out with great care.

Although our plans aimed at the early completion of the promenade saloon, thought was already being given to the problems of the restoration of the after dining saloon. Our research had revealed that, unusually, the planking of the dining saloon deck was laid athwartship, using boards four inches thick. This deck is almost at the level of the waterline, and it is assumed that Brunel used the deck planking to act as a structural membrane, giving the ship beam strength. These planks were bolted to plate stringers which remain at the ship's sides, but they must also have been supported by fore and aft timbers with pillars to the hold deck below. Also remaining at this level when the ship returned home were more T bulb beams of 1882, all in excellent condition. After considering various options, we decided to begin by laying a steel deck of quarter-inch plate, supported by the existing beams; comparatively thin planks could then be used to lay an athwartship deck. This decision gave the slight advantage of additional protection in the event of a fire in the hold below, where we plan to install heating and ventilating plant at a later date, and we also realised that the plate underlay would provide an ideal support for the portable scaffolding needed by the craftsmen fastening the planking of the promenade deck. As a result this work was brought forward, meaning that the wood decking of the dining level can quickly follow the completion of the promenade saloon.

At last all the preliminaries had been completed, and the planking of the promenade saloon deck began early in 1985. To simplify the task and reduce cost, the deck was laid as a close boarded floor without caulking, but each plank still had to be secured by coach screws passing through holes drilled in the beams below. At first our finances were so stretched that the work had to be planned in stages, the first of which was to complete an area of deck at the forward end of the saloon by July, when a visit by the Queen was expected. Who better to be the first visitor to tread the new deck? It is often said that a royal visit introduces a touch of magic, which may explain why this one coincided with a dramatic change of fortune. As a result it was possible to continue the decking of the promenade saloon virtually without a break, until its completion in the spring of 1986.

Now our attention was focused on the design and installation of the many and various features of the promenade saloon—stairways, bulkheads, doorways and the steering mechanism housed in its own enclosure at the after end of the stern gallery. Fortunately, contemporary deck plans have survived, but while the production of a general arrangement drawing presented few problems, the interpretation of details of individual items occupied many hours of discussion by the ship committee. As has been noted, the trunk of the lifting propeller system was cut down only to the level of the promenade deck, so a substantial section of it remains in the ship, in a space originally filled by a double stairway connecting the two saloons. This will be impossible to restore, but to preserve the original appearance of the stern gallery we have introduced stairway openings with balusters and rails and the top of two dummy stairways. At the dining saloon level the absence of the after entrance has had to be accepted, but two steel emergency exit stairways have been planned to link the two saloons, screened behind the cabin frontages.

At the promenade level the screen bulkheads forming the frontages of the cabin blocks are now in place, and when the passageway doors are in position the illusion will be created that everything is in place. At least one block of four cabins is to be restored as a public exhibit, and the ladies' boudoir or state room on the port side will also be re-created. At the forward end of the saloon the Captain's day cabin, which also served as a chart room, will be fully restored and furnished. The passengers' water closets were at the upper 'tween level to port and starboard of the engine compartment, and there are plans to restore at least one of these for inspection only!

Apart from walking the decks and playing cards, the passengers were able to enjoy such diversions as watching the crew working the sails, peering through the engine room skylight for the reassuring sight of the machinery revolving, and even staring out of the stern gallery windows at the churning wake, with the clanking of steering gear chains in their ears. With the ship sitting in a Bristol dry dock it is impossible to appreciate the full physical experience of crossing the Atlantic in such a relatively small vessel, especially the acute discomforts that accompany rough weather! But we hope that, when all is complete as planned, an imaginative visitor will be able to glimpse at least a hint of the life of a transatlantic passenger enjoying the luxuries of the period.

19—'One Door Closes'

In 1985 what I called the rebuilding phase had virtually come to an end. Apart from the engine, which was still almost a project in its own right, the rest of the restoration work could be grouped under the shipyard description of 'fitting out'. This seemed a logical time for a change of management, and I asked the project council to arrange for me to be relieved of my responsibilities before the end of 1986. There was a surprising number of applicants to fill my post but at last, in November 1986, Captain Chris Young R.N. (Retired) assumed the position I had occupied for more than 16 years. In fact I was surprised to reflect that after completing 32 years of naval service I had subsequently served more than half that time in only one ship! My wife added her own light-hearted comment to the effect that for the first years of our marriage she had shared me with a grey mistress, and for the next 16 with a black one!

Looking back to the beginning, it is true to say that success hung on the thread of public support. Although solvent, the project lacked the funds even to begin serious restoration work, and all the facilities for visitors had to be improvised. Fortunately, this did not discourage the British public, and by coming in their thousands they both contributed essential funds and gave a much-needed boost to our morale. From then on we never lost confidence, but it was to be many years before our restoration programme, like the national economy, ceased to operate on a stop/go system, as progress was tailored rigidly to available finance.

I suppose the first turning point in the care of the ship came with the employment of our first maintenance worker, or shipkeeper, as he was originally called. From this small beginning our maintenance team has slowly expanded to the point that it is now headed by a retired chief engineer, and includes a rigger, an electrician and a boilermaker in its ranks. Tribute must also be given to our team of voluntary workers who devote most of their Sundays to caring for the ship, organised by their long-standing leader, Max Osborne.

A major administrative milestone for the project was the retirement of Richard Goold-Adams from the office of chairman, and his replacement by Dr. Basil Greenhill, who brought into our deliberations all his wide experience and knowledge of maritime history, a result of both a lifetime of study and his recent service as Director of the National Maritime Museum in Greenwich. It could be said that this change came at an opportune time, when Richard had virtually completed the tedious task of laying sure foundations for the ship's future, leaving Basil the task of building on them.

Throughout restoration we have been constantly bedevilled by a lack of detailed contemporary information, and this especially applied to the finer points of the interior layout and decoration. Here everything depended on the correct interpretation of written descriptions and sketches. The ship committee was not qualified to adjudicate on such details, so Dr. Greenhill formed a new committee of experts, the development committee, whose task it would be to sift all the evidence and make recommendations on details of decoration and furnishings. Their deliberations have allowed decisions to be made on the design, layout and colour of the elaborate decorative scheme of the promenade saloon, work on which should soon begin.

After years of happy partnership with Tim Webb, I was sad when he reached retiring age, and the first break in our original management team had to be made. We were fortunate to gain the services of Brian Wheddon, who has continued to develop the commercial components of our enterprise so ably established by Tim. Soon after this change it was at last possible to allocate funds to begin some long-planned improvements to the primitive amenities for visitors. In the old building on the north side of the dock a modern system of entry control was installed in a newly designed entrance, and a spacious souvenir shop was established astride the exit. Above all, we were able to meet a long-felt want with the introduction of a video display facility beside the entrance, where the visitors now receive a preliminary briefing to add to the interest and enjoyment of their tour of the ship.

Over the years the most commonly asked question was 'when will it be finished?' Once the initial euphoria had evaporated, many perhaps thought that the answer would be 'never', but after a few years it was my habit to say 'within ten years, given the money!'

Now that sufficient funds are available to complete the planned task, progress is regulated by other factors, including the need to allow daily access to visitors; but at the time of writing, completion in the early 1990s seems reasonably certain. Of course work will not end then, because maintenance will go on forever, and there will always be some interesting activity for the visitor to see. It is also almost inevitable that as the current plans reach fruition, fresh proposals could add new items, such as the galley and crew's quarters amidships, even the conversion of the forward hold into an exhibition centre.

What is certain is that the heady days of independence, when even the future home of the ship lay in the balance, are gone forever. The future lies in an ever closer relationship with the development of the leisure facilities around the old Bristol City Docks, while preserving the project's identity and basic aim. Apart from becoming a major exhibit and an important national industrial landmark, the ship is gradually becoming accepted as a prestigious venue for social events. These help swell the essential income which will always be needed to cover the high cost of maintenance, but the project remains committed to the preservation of the nineteenth-century atmosphere and features of the original interior, and is determined to resist any attempt at commercial exploitation.

As always, the true reward for all our efforts is the sight of a succession of visitors from all parts of the world inspecting and applauding what has been achieved. The student of naval architecture has a special interest in a ship that provides

The author, with Dr. Greenhill, explains the working of the cable stoppers to H.M. The Queen.

a living demonstration of the beginnings of the methods of construction fundamental to his profession. Similarly, with the completion of the engine, it can be expected that marine engineers will begin to beat a path to the door.

As a schoolboy I was especially fascinated by the achievements of the Victorian engineers, but little thought how closely I was to become involved in them, and especially with the work of I.K. Brunel. After more than 16 years as custodian of his second maritime success, I have no hesitation in reaffirming the importance of the *Great Britain* both as a part of our maritime and industrial heritage and as a major milestone on the road of shipbuilding.

Our country, and indeed the world, owes a debt of gratitude to the dedicated men who formed the original project committee, and faced the incredible task of rescue from that far-off shore in the Falkland Islands.